SIN

JENNIFER JULIE MILLER

Acknowledgments

I want to dedicate this book to my husband, **Rick.** There are no words to describe my love for you, but the one thing I really want to say is, thank you, for WANTING me, and for being my HERO!

Also, I want to say thanks to my parents, my amazing kids, my beautiful grandkids, my crazy aunt, and all my friends for all your constant support. I want to thank my family for all the hours you have had to listen to the insane ideas inside my head. Even though most of you think I need to be evaluated.

Cover Art by © Creative cover Designs
(Vicki Adrian) Artist

Beta Readers:
Lorene Palmer, Rick Miller, Ethel Nance.
Editors:
Partners in Crime Book Services, Randy Henry.
Photographs:
Brittany Henry & Rick Miller, Shutterstock, Adobe stock
photos.
Imaginational inspiration crew:
Jewel Shipley, Amanda Hall, Joann Herley, Vicki Adrian.

Chapter One

SiN

WHILE APPROACHING the outer perimeter of the Dark Forest of Darverius, my vision begins to blur as my body starts to shut down. This results in me coming in too fast, landing my shuttle rougher than intended, jerking my already injured body hard against the seat restraints. Instinctively, I reach up, opening the viewer, setting the sensors on high alert until the engine's power down fully. Hoping no one saw that amateur landing before my ship had time to cloak itself.

As MY EYES search for any threats awaiting me outside, I try to gather my thoughts now that I have escaped Targres Four.

The intense pain radiating through me tells me that I require a healer, but revealing my true self to anyone on this planet is not an option. In my present condition, I'm not in any shape to fight off the many enemies I have acquired. Frack, I can barely move, let alone anything else.

GRITTING MY TEETH, it takes everything I have not to scream out in agony as my skin feels like it is being boiled off my bones from the inside out. Taking a deep breath, I do my best to push the pain away. I wait for the ship to finish camouflaging itself so I can get out without giving up its location. The last thing I need right now is to lose my ship, especially now, knowing they are hunting for me.

HAVING the latest stealth technology installed into my shuttle took the last of the credits I stole from Targres Four. However, right this moment, I wish I had spent a small portion of it on an internal healing chamber instead. As prepared as I try to be for most circumstances, I didn't foresee this. Once I'm healed, that will be the next thing on my list to acquire for my ship.

WHAT SKIN I can see through smoke-filled, swollen eyes is blackened and blistered. The majority of my right side seems to be burned, some places worse than others. Fortunately, my cloak managed to block most of my body from further injury. As that bastard clipped me just as I was turning away.

I'm still puzzled as to how they found me so quickly. Especially since I tampered with the sensors and the cameras located at the gate where I took the female. Thankfully, I anticipated the odds that someone might show up at the warehouse and took precautions in case things went wrong. Frack, did they go wrong?

Lord of Light knows that orange bastard, my so-called brother, did a number on me, but I had the last laugh in the end. There is no way any of them survived that bomb at such close range.

I smile, even though it's painful, wondering how dear old Dad will handle the loss of two of his chosen ones. With that thought, apparently, the research I have gathered on all my so-called brothers is not as accurate as I assumed. Because nowhere did it say ViN could throw fireballs at lava-like temperatures from the palms of his hands. Nor did it mention that he had mated the human female I took from the compound.

. . .

THIS IS something I need to look further into. If I had known any of this in advance, I never would have contacted the Jynrel with the sale of that female and all of this could have been prevented.

THE CREDITS that human female was worth at the time was more tempting than the consequences of being caught, or so I thought until now. My well-thought-out plan to destroy my father and all he holds dear is quickly unraveling, and now because of these injuries. I'm having to waste time to heal before I can contemplate my next step. Right now, all I can concentrate on is getting somewhere safe before my body shuts down completely. I'll have to figure the rest out later.

THE AGONY COURSING through me has made my mind fuzzy. I can't remember the last time I was injured to this extent. I know there are a few supplies stocked inside of Mystic that might help with the pain until my natural healing kicks in, but right now, she seems to be a great distance away, especially in the shape I'm in.

THE BURNING IS SO intense it has my entire body shaking and disoriented, making it hard for me to pull the handle for the ramp to extend down. Stumbling out the door, I barely remember to hit the control panel for the ramp to close. Once the ship is secure. I try to mist, only for the pain to drop me to my knees. Kneeling there for a moment, gasping. I try to figure out what to do now since I can't hold the misted form I normally travel.

Getting to my feet, I hesitantly head into the darkness, trying my best to avoid the many Seline patrolling the area. This proves much harder to do on foot and is something I'm not familiar with as I usually mist past them. After a few close calls, I finally make it to Mystic's base. My only genuine friend, and the oldest guardian of her kind. I've developed an attachment to the colossal tree that gazes upon my father's residence.

Initially, I had no idea she was a guardian or that sentient trees existed. I thought it was simply luck that led me to what has become my only home. It took several risings of things moving around me before I realized she was alive. I have only heard her soft voice a few times, but her extreme presence can't be missed. She has protected me and sheltered me when I had nothing and nowhere to go. This rising, I'm in desperate need of her comforting arms.

. . .

LEANING AGAINST HER VAST TRUNK, I take several deep breaths, dreading the toll it's going to take on my body to mist up into the safe haven she has always provided for me. Clenching my teeth, I will my body to fragment, but I can't hold back the painful scream that echoes out around me as my body separates into millions of burned and broken pieces.

I'M ONLY HALFWAY up to my sacred hiding spot when I start to lose my form. The pain seems to triple as my body reforms. Helpless, I feel myself falling when suddenly, one of Mystic's large limbs grabs onto me, pushing me the rest of the way up. Stumbling onto the floor of the only home I have had in rotations, I fall to my back, panting for breath. I know I need to get these clothes off and treat my wounds, but I don't have the strength or the power to move.

MYSTIC CLOSES HER LIMBS, surrounding me in the blessed darkness of her foliage, and I close my eyes. I must have passed out from the pain when an odd scent suddenly awakens me. I know immediately that someone or something has invaded my sanctuary. Instinctively, I reach out, only to find my hand closing around a slender neck.

A GASP HAS me forcing my eyes open. My haven has been contaminated by another. An angel with violet eyes and a bruised face. The female jerks away from me and before I can grab onto her, she trips on the cloak she is wearing. Arms flailing, she unknowingly tumbles out of the opening Mystic has sheltered us in.

HER SCREAM IS QUICKLY SILENCED, and this bothers me more than it should. After all, how dare she come into my home uninvited? Grunting, I manage to roll over onto my uninjured side and crawl forward. I dread seeing her broken body on the ground far below. I don't know who is more shocked at the scene below, me or the female. She is being cradled gently within one of Mystic's massive limbs.

I EXPECT Mystic to set her down and push her away from us. However, once again, she shocks me when I see her bringing the girl back up slowly.

"MYSTIC, WHAT ARE YOU DOING?" Not expecting an answer, I have to catch myself against the wall when her voice whispers gently around me.

"YOUNGLING, you're not the only one without shelter and lost. You need not concern yourself with the female. You should rest and heal, for your journey has just begun."

. . .

I start to open my mouth to argue, only for my entire body to fold up under me, and I fall back to the floor. Blessed darkness pushes the pain to only haunt my dreams.

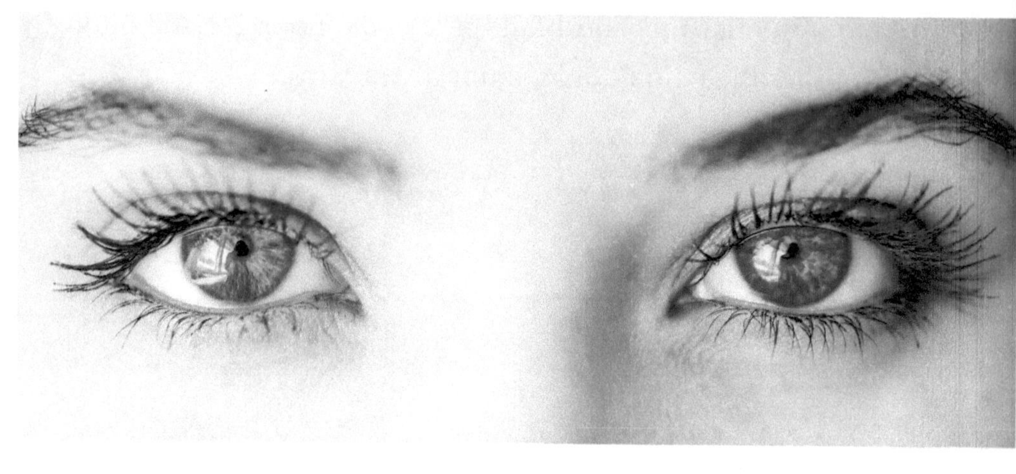

Chapter Two

Ellaria

A NEW PRESENCE has made itself known in my sacred forest. For unknown reasons, I'm drawn to it as it moves all over the area in no particular direction. Thorn walks quietly at my side as we make our way towards the unique smell that has the entire forest buzzing.

SUDDENLY, I sense something nearby. A mind swirling as it awakens to a blankness of unknowing. A brain seeking answers with no emotions behind it. I look around, but my eyes cannot locate its source. I have never come upon one such as this, and now my inquisitiveness is piqued.

. . .

THORN GROWLS SOFTLY, pushing against me, as he puts himself between me and whatever has disturbed his heightened senses. My corporeal form flickers with his unease and that's when I notice a different texture laying within inches of us on the ground.

WHEN IT WHIMPERS, I float back, allowing Thorn to push me further away, but my curiosity won't allow me to go far. When that pitiful sound left the creature lying on the ground hidden from me. Something inside of me demands that I protect whatever it is.

THORN MUST FEEL the same way as he barks out a warning to the Selin headed towards us. They too must have heard the soft whimper that is so out of place in their world, and were coming to investigate. Cautiously, Thorn nudges the small camouflage lump with his snout, and it curls up, pulling its covering tighter against its slight form.

THORN BARKS again and the creature jerks, a pale foot appears on the ground in front of me, only to be hastily pulled back under the covering. This magical disguise is the only thing that has saved this delicate creature from being discovered by the beast that lingers within the dark forest.

WITHOUT WARNING, I watch as it rises. It doesn't even look around, just simply starts running. Following behind, I glide effortlessly above the ground, staying as close as I can without gaining its attention. Thorn even backs off slightly, using the trees to hide his substantial form.

ABRUPTLY, it stops, cowering next to one of the younger Guardian's trunks. That's when I saw … her. A delicate, pale, but bruised face peeks out of the covering. She glances my way, but it's like she is unsteady and unfocused, to the point she isn't trusting her eyes. She sways unsteadily on her feet, and that's when I feel it … confusion.

HER LACK of fear stems from her ignorance of her surroundings. Thorn makes a grunting noise behind me. She jumps, startled by the sound, then takes off running in no particular direction. I follow her deeper into the forest, watching some of the Guardians look down, puzzled themselves about the strange creature darting through them so carelessly.

. . .

HER THOUGHTS and emotions are fragmented, but she can't hide the pain that is overwhelming her mind. She is hungry, cold, and mutely terrified. I motion for Thorn to lead her towards Mystic. I know the Guardian will shelter and keep her safe until I can get help.

THORN GROWLS, and she trips a couple of times, running as fast as she can until I can tell she is at the point of collapsing. Falling against Mystic's massive base. She turns, looking around for another way to go. When she doesn't find it, I don't know who is more shocked, me or Mystic, when she starts to climb.

MYSTIC FORMS small indentions for her to hold on to unknowingly to the female. All of us are impressed with her will to live and what she is willing to do to escape and survive. However, the further up she goes, the slower she is getting. I can't tell if it's from fear or her unknown injuries.

MYSTIC CAN FEEL her grip lessening as her small body shakes with the strain it's taking to pull herself up. I watch from below as Mystic moves a limb under her in case she starts to slip, but the female doesn't seem to notice the massive limbs rearranging themselves underneath her.

· · ·

RISING UP, I hover right behind her, momentarily lost in what to do to help. Glancing down at Thorn, who is pacing in front of Mystic's base, it hits me. I lean forward, touching her unknowingly on the back, willing the strength I'm pulling from Thorn into her. She gasps, but starts to scramble up the tree. Finally, crawling into the hollowed-out sanctuary in Mystic that is far above the ground, and safe from all the predators below.

I WATCH as she scrambles all the way to the back, whimpering as she collapses onto her knees, instinctively pulling the cloak tighter around her before she falls over in exhaustion. Since she has pushed her body as far as it will go, it doesn't take long for her breathing to even out. As soon as she is asleep, Mystic forms soft bedding under her, then covers her more securely with the leaves from her canopy.

I TOUCH the wall willing my voice into the wood around me, hoping Mystic can still hear my thoughts as she had gone to ground Orbital rotations ago. "Old friend, I apologize for bringing her here. For some reason, I simply could not let her perish below."

"ELLARIA, earlier, her presence awakened me. I knew she would end up here, eventually. She will need things I cannot provide her. She is different from the others I have sheltered before. I need you to see if you can procure the things it will take to sustain her. For now, I will make sure she rests. Her mind is clouded, but I believe with the right care, the small female's body will heal. I fear her mind will take much longer."

"Oh Mystic, my dearest friend, it is so good to hear your voice. I'm glad you have come out of your roots and back into your trunk. We have been in need of your guidance for quite some time now … Mystic, what if SiN shows up while she is here? He will not be kind."

"That male is lost inside his own mind. I will intervene if he arrives. No harm shall come to her now that she is in my care."

"Forgive me, I should have known you already anticipated this as well. You are right, Mystic. She needs things that neither of us can comprehend. There is one that lives within the forest I believe will understand her needs. I will approach her and ask for her assistance in this matter. I will return as quickly as possible."

Chapter Three

Ellaria

REFORMING IN FRONT OF THORN, we quickly head towards the only dwelling located inside the dark forest. I don't know how she always knows I'm close by, but I no more than step out of the cover of darkness when the door opens.

"HELLO ELLARIA."

"KATHERINE." I hesitate, as I'm not sure exactly how to ask her for the things I require.

. . .

"Ellaria, I can feel your unease, is there something you need from me?"

"How do you know I have need of you?"

"It's hard to explain, it's a combination of things, really. Thorn's emotions and feelings are always floating around in the back of my mind, and I knew he was headed this way. Most of the time, I can feel your presence in the forest, sometimes more intensely than others. However, I don't seek you out because I'm well aware that you find extreme emotions overwhelming and that's why you stay away. Honestly, I was shocked to suddenly feel your need to speak to me so strongly."

"You are correct in your assumptions, Katherine. I am on a mission and I do need your assistance, as I have no actual knowledge of others in the flesh. There is a female of your species who is in hardship, and I believe she will require comforts and substance. Can you provide me with those things, or should I seek the counsel of another?"

"Where? Lead me to her and I will have RaZ or one of the others bring her back here."

. . .

KATHERINE'S EMOTIONS hit me hard, and I have to force myself not to fade. "I'm sorry, but at this time, that's not possible. Her fate is tied to another, and I can't let you sever that bond before it has had time to form. She is weak, in mind and body, right now, but we hope to tend to her with your guidance."

"SO YOU ARE TELLING me you are hiding her for your gain, not her own?"

"No … and yes. She is the only one who holds the light that might dampen the hatred in the darkest of hearts. If she is removed, all hope is lost, and I won't allow you or any other to take away his possibility of redemption. If you will not assist me, I will seek it elsewhere." I start to turn away.

"No, Ellaria. I will take your word that she will be taken care of, for now, and I will help in any way I can. You said she needs stuff. Can you be more specific?"

"SHE HAS NOTHING."

. . .

"WELL, that helps. Can I ask the others for assistance?"

"I'D RATHER YOU NOT. I know I'm asking a lot from you, Katherine, but I need your absolute silence on this matter for now. Her path as it's clouded in mystery, but I know she is crucial to healing the darkness and hatred that encloses his heart."

SHE STANDS there looking at me, her hands on her hips, and I can tell she is working through the information I have told her.

"OK, since I don't know what size she is, clothes will be slightly difficult, but the rest shouldn't be a problem."

"SHE IS SLIGHT OF BUILD, similar to yourself."

"OK, that does help. Would you like to come inside while I gather a few things?"

I START TO SAY NO, but something stops me. With every rising, I have become more fascinated with the differences this race of females are changing in the world around me. Their small bodies hold an array of emotions and strengths many can't comprehend. Thorn nudges me from behind, then walks off towards the other large hounds that have been lying patiently around Katherine's feet while we have been talking.

KATHERINE DOESN'T WAIT to see if I am going to follow her. She leaves the door open as she walks away. Floating in behind her hesitantly, I take the time to look around the structure, amazed at how different it looks on the inside. I knew there was a cloak hiding its true form outside, but I never expected this. Large decorative archways branch off the multiple floors, heading to places unseen from below. Paintings and carved designs cover the stone walls as the large turrets reach towards the sky. The dwelling feels open and inviting like a dwelling should if I had ever had one of my own.

KATHERINE APPEARS ABOVE, and I'm immediately curious as to how she got there so quickly without any wings. As it's obvious, this dwelling was designed for RaZ specifically with all of its ledges.

"IT'S JUST US, Ellaria. Come on up. RaZ was called away; something is going on with Solanar."

. . .

I DON'T TELL her I already know he is gone. RaZ's emotions are powerful and easily detected, so it was effortless for me to determine his absence. She jumps slightly when I simply appear right in front of her.

"ELLARIA, that's quite the handy little trick you have there. I could use that superpower, that's for sure. Let's go see what I can scrounge up for our mystery girl. My only other question is, how are you going to get this to wherever you are headed?"

"I HAVE a question of my own first. How did you appear above me that quickly without wings yourself?"

"OH, that's an easy one. RaZ put an elevator in for all of us not blessed with wings or floating superpowers."

"HUMM, interesting. The things we will do to comfort our loved ones seem never-ending, and to answer your other question, even though he will not like it, I was going to have Thorn carry the items for me."

. . .

"OH, he might fuss some, but I'm sure deep down he won't mind. However, I need to keep that in mind and not pack the bags too heavily. It may be easier for me to send things a few times a day, especially food and stuff."

"I DIDN'T CONSIDER the fact that she would need substance every rising."

"YEAH, on this side of the realm, we require many things to keep us going. I'll send food with one of the hounds daily so that you won't have to worry about her going hungry. Now, does she need any first aid stuff?"

"WHAT IS THIS FIRST AID?"

"IS SHE HURT?"

"I'M NOT SURE, I believe she is, but I don't think it is anything life-threatening. I could feel her pain, but I didn't actually see her physical body. She was hidden from me by a covering I can't explain. Can you provide assistance without seeing her?"

. . .

"WELL, since you won't tell me where she is, we're gonna have to hope for the best. She has made it this far, after all. I will send what I have here along with you. Most of it is self-explanatory. She should be able to figure it out. I believe in one of these packs there may even be a small handheld healer for minor cuts and abrasions that will help, too. I'll have to reset the language though, so that she can read the instructions. The device is extremely handy to have around for most minor injuries."

WHILE KATHERINE BUZZES around the room full of clothing and accessories, I hover back out of the way. A pile of things seems to get larger every time she opens a drawer, or comes back into the room. After a few moments, she stops, a frown on her face.

"OK, I may have to rethink this, is it ok if I send Ghost with you too? That way, she could have most of everything she might need right away."

"THAT SHOULD BE FINE."

SHE ROLLS and tucks things inside several bags. Then motions for me to follow her into another chamber. She fills the rest of the bags to the point where she almost can't close them with substance.

"THIS SHOULD DO her for a few days. I'll have Alana design a harness to fit Thorn this evening, so the bags don't bother him. Do you think we may be doing this for a while?"

"KATHERINE, so many things are unknown to me right now, but I know this is not a permanent situation. However, I can't see the outcome at this moment."

THE NEED TO return to Mystic begins to bother me. Something tells me that I will be needed soon and that I need to hurry. I have to fight myself to stay, as I'm being pulled back aggressively. "Katherine, I won't be able to remain much longer, something is coming."

KATHERINE DOESN'T LINGER any longer. She grabs the bags and we both head outside where the hounds are awaiting us. Then she drapes the two large bags over Thorn and Ghost's backs, both of them growling lightly, their fur bristling in annoyance at their weight.

· · ·

"Oh, stop it both of you, it's only for a few minutes, both of you have carried heavier items many times over. Keida rides Raven all the time and you don't hear her complaining."

I NOD my head in thanks, no longer able to talk as my form simply fades away. I race towards Mystic. Thorn, and Ghost, running swiftly behind me even with the heavy bags on their backs.

WHEN I FINALLY MAKE IT to Mystic's base, the emotions happening all around me bombard my mind. The pain is making it hard for me to move forward. I hear the female scream and I feel her fear as she tumbles backward out of the hollowed opening inside of Mystic's trunk. Helpless, I can do nothing but watch as she falls quickly towards the forest floor and her death.

SECONDS before she hits the ground, Mystic reaches one of her largest limbs out, catching her just in time. Mystic is hurting, and the female is terrified, but it's the agony of another that engulfs my mind. It takes all of my strength to look up and when I do. I see a set of eyes that would match my own if I had survived the flesh. SiN, my twin brother.

· · ·

HE DOESN'T NOTICE ME, he only has eyes for the female, who in his mind has invaded his sanctuary. Mystic struggles to lift the girl up as she herself hasn't moved freely in Orbital rotations. Her massive limbs and trunk have been stationary for so long that she is having a hard time maneuvering their immense weight. She lifts the female as carefully as she can, ungracefully tossing her back into the opening before closing the area off more solidly.

PUSHING ALL THE EMOTIONS AWAY, I quickly follow behind, only to find SiN passed out on the floor and the female cowering over in the corner, trembling. She doesn't scream or make a sound when I appear, even though I know she can now see me. It's like her mind is a blank slate, and she doesn't know what to fear.

THE AGONY COMING from SiN's unconscious form practically has me doubling over, but I push through it when I hear Thorn growling aggressively outside. Sending my thoughts towards him, he settles down waiting for me at Mystic's base.

SENDING MY THOUGHTS OUT, "Mystic … Thorn and the other hound have brought some supplies. I believe there may even be some healing items inside the bags. Are you able to bring them up here?"

. . .

"Ellaria, I have remained in this position for so long it's like I'm having to figure out how to move again like a young sapling. It may take me a few moments, but I will retrieve the items you have acquired. SiN is badly injured, and I put him into a healing sleep to escape any further harm to his body. I was worried he would do more damage to himself if I didn't."

Looking down at his ravaged and burned body, I whisper. "Oh my poor lost brother, what have you done now?"

Chapter Four

Jade

What's wrong? Why am I so confused? There seems to be nothing but a huge blank spot in my mind. I have no idea where I'm at, or even how I got to wherever this is. I just woke up here in the dark, it's like I didn't exist before this moment. There is nothing but a void with no memories.

Suddenly, the sound of odd, scratchy angry voices surrounding me alerts me to the danger I'm in, and I push back further into the darkness. *"This thing is dangerous, I've heard rumors that their blood is even poisonous, there are not enough credits out there worth getting caught with this thing. We have to dispose of it quickly."*

SOMETHING HITS the side of this crate, or room, hard, and I scream out, ducking down. All I hear after that is laughter as they walk away. Since then, there has been nothing but long periods of extreme silence in a place so dark I can't see my hand in front of my face. The only constant noise is the sound of my stomach growling and my own heart beat as I can feel myself weakening quickly.

I CATCH MYSELF DOZING OFF, as there isn't anything else to do besides sleep when out of the blue something sharp stabs me in the leg. I don't even have time to scream out from the shock or the pain that something roughly lifts me up. Tossing me around and around as it wraps some sort of fabric tightly round me.

EVEN THOUGH THEIR words are hard to make out because of all the chaos they openly talk around me like I can't under-stand them. *"This is the plan. It should perish quickly out there, as small as it is. This covering I stole will keep anyone from seeing us pack it through the clearing to dispose of it. Even if it's found, there is no way they can track it back to us."*

. . .

THE MATERIAL HAS BECOME SO CONSTRICTING I start to smother. Crying out, I fight against the casing they have placed me in, until multiple hands suddenly begin to swing me back and forth. Weightlessly, I'm thrown aggressively through the air.

MY BODY HITS HARD, face first, against the unforgiving ground as I tumble over and over inside this wrapping. When I finally come to a stop. The tears flow rapidly down my face as I fight to free myself of this thing that is restraining me. Kicking and screaming, I finally break free. Panting for breath, I look around trying not to panic at the unknown sight in front of me. I'm in some type of misty, dark forest.

SOMEHOW, I know I have never seen or been anywhere like this before. The trees tower so far above my head that I can't see the top of the canopy. Everything is cloaked in a darkness that seems to absorb every ounce of light possible. I whirl around when I hear the sound of voices behind me. Blindly, unknowing anything about my surroundings. I scramble to my feet, running as fast as I can in the other direction. I won't let them take me back.

PURE WILL POWER is all that is pushing me forward towards a destination I don't know of. When I can no longer hear anyone behind me, I stop. Taking a second to catch my breath, and look around. If I could just find a place to hide, it would give me time to figure out what to do next.

THEN IT DAWNS ON ME, the trees, there has to be a place I can hide in one of them. I have never seen a forest or trees such as these before, but this place has to have animals thriving within it. Once I find shelter, I'm sure there is some type of fruit or something I will be able to find to eat.

WOUND UP in my own thoughts I almost miss the deep growl behind me. My mind immediately conjures up the worst things imaginable. Without looking back, I take off running again, stumbling along as my feet are being shredded upon the rough surface of the forest floor beneath them. Tears flow freely down my face as I fall several more times over things I can't clearly see in the dusty darkness of the forest around me, but I refuse to stop. Each time I hit the ground I have to make myself get back up and keep going.

HOWEVER, the feeling of something watching me has me pushing through the last of my strength as I sprint forward. Glancing around as I run through the woods, I swear it looks like the trees are moving out of my way, but trees don't move. Or do they? I don't know, I'm so confused. Thinking has become too draining, so I push all the unknown to the side. Right now, I can't lose focus. I have to find a place to stop, some place no one can find me.

TRIPPING UPON ANOTHER ROOT. I find myself at the base of the largest tree I have ever seen, it's so massive there is no seeing around it. *Where do I go now?* I study the tree trunk for a moment, admiring the huge limbs above me. That's when it dawns on me, if I can get up to one of those limbs, I could take a moment to rest. They are so high up, I should be able to see anything else around.

THE GROWLS GETTING CLOSER MAKE my decision for me. I tie the material I had been clutching this whole time around my neck and reach up. Tucking my hands securely into the small cracks running up and down this vast tree trunk.

PUSHING past the pain of my fingernails ripping, I wince when my weight settles up on my torn feet. When I start slipping, I make myself stop and lean against the tree. Trying not to look up or down, as I don't aspire to be discouraged either way.

THANKFULLY, I have been able to find easier hand holds the further up I go, but I'm so tired. Tears flow down my face as my body shakes in exhaustion. Another growl below me gives me the extra energy I need to push myself up, and before I realize it. I come upon a hollowed-out opening and it takes the last of my strength to pull myself inward. Once inside, I take a second to look around hoping there isn't anything else in here but me. Relieved when I find myself alone.

THE INTERIOR of the tree seems slightly warmer than the forest floor, as its large leaves are blocking the wind and the crispness of the air outside. Scrambling on hands and knees, I head towards the back, trying to get as far as I can away from the terrors that have followed me through the forest. Leaning back against the strong but steady wall of the tree, I whisper. "Thank you for your shelter, You have no idea how grateful I am to have found your secret spot."

WRAPPING the covering back around me, I allow myself a minute to fall apart before exhaustion claims me in a deep sleep. I don't know what wakes me up, but suddenly, I know I'm no longer alone. Opening my eyes slowly, I peek out of the covering. Thankfully there is just enough light coming through the trees' hollowed-out opening to see and there is no missing the gigantic figure lying a few feet in front of me.

· · ·

I WATCH it for a little bit and, when it doesn't move, I slowly get to my torn feet, walking cautiously towards it, ready to run at the first sign of movement. Drawn by some unknown force, I find myself leaning over … him.

I HAVE NEVER SEEN anything like him before. Even with my memories as scattered as they are, I know he's not human, but his features are similar, only sharper. His breathing seems labored, and his face is scrunched up in pain.

MY HAND HESITATES over his chest, the contours appearing almost artificial in their perfection. The discipline and strength necessary to shape a body like this is beyond my imagination. I'm so caught up in admiring his physique in this dim light that I almost miss the burns and injuries on his side opposite of me.

I MUST HAVE MADE some sort of noise because the next thing I know, he grasps me around the neck. Out of the pure will to live, I immediately start to fight against his hold, but not before his bright yellow eyes seem to burn their way into my soul. Yanking hard, his hand drops away, and I stagger backward with his sudden release.

. . .

My arms swing outward as I try to catch myself from falling right out the opening I was so happy to find earlier. A terrorized scream leaves my throat as I plummet towards the ground. Seconds from death, something swoops in underneath me. Catching me roughly within a hard but giving surface.

The fall knocks the breath out of me, and my skin tears where it impacts the limb, but I'm still alive. My hands fly out, grasping onto the limb that is suddenly moving beneath me. Rising me higher, back towards the hole I just fell out of, and the massive male who was not happy to find me there.

It dumps me not so gently inside and then closes the opening. I back up against the wall, trying to get as far away as I can from the male slumped over on his side in front of me. His labored breathing shows how badly he is hurt, but my own tortured body is not in much better shape.

A dim light unexpectedly appears in front of me. The apparition that emerges out of that light has me doubting my senses and my mind, as there is no way this … she is real.

Chapter Five

Jade

My mind might be fuzzy, and if my eyes are not completely deceiving me, I believe that the beautiful creature flickering in and out, hovering above the floor is a ghost. She is focused on the male lying on the floor, and doesn't seem to notice that I'm here,

My whole body seems like it's shaking. *What in the hell just happened? What the hell is going on and who the hell are these people...things? How the hell did I get here?* I feel like my mind is about to snap. Something terrible has happened to me and either I am blocking it all, or...worse.

. . .

PULLING the covering over my naked form closer, I close my eyes. Seeking a single moment of silence in this chaos. Even dazed I know this is something I have done my entire life, praying for peace. When everything else has failed me my faith that there was a path I was meant to be on has never swayed. There has to be a reason for my memory loss, but do I want to remember what it is … or was?

FEELING something brush against my cheek, I jerk back, opening my eyes. A small, dainty hand hovers in front of me. Drifting a few feet back, she must have seen the panic in my eyes. She tries to say something, but I can't understand her. When I don't respond, she tries again.

"I'M sorry if I scared you more than you already are, but it appears there might be an issue with your translator. Or it's possible it could have been installed incorrectly, as you should have been able to understand my native language. Lucky for you, I have listened enough to the others that your language has become embedded into my consciousness.

"YOU HAVE nothing to fear from me. I promise I'm not here to hurt you. This will probably seem somewhat odd to you.

Well, other than the obvious." She points towards herself. "But I felt your presence in the forest earlier and followed you here. You have to be hungry and would probably appreciate some clothing. Even in this form, I prefer to be covered. We all have things that make us more comfortable. Often I change the design of my clothing to suit my mood.

"MYSTIC AND I have acquired some personal items for you, she will bring them up shortly. I don't know your story, but Mystic has told me and the other Guardians that you were seeking sanctuary and it has been granted. Nothing will bother you while in their protection here in the forest."

"WHO IS MYSTIC, and what are you?" I whisper out.

"FORGIVE ME. My manners are not as well formed as they should be. I am Ellaria, this forest is my home, and the one you are being sheltered within," she motions around us with her arms, "is Mystic. She is the oldest Guardian of her kind and has watched over Darverius since the beginning of time. May I ask your name?"

SHE HOVERS away from me and closer to the guy who is still lying on his side, as I think of the question she just asks me.

My name, Ughh. I know I have a name. I can hear others calling me by it. Suddenly, a picture of an older man pops in my head. He is playing with me, swinging me around in his arms laughing. It takes me a second to relive this event, that's when I hear it." My name is Becca. Becca Jade Simpson, but I believe my friends call me Jade."

"I WOULD BE HONORED to call you that as well."

AN OPENING APPEARS in the wall and two small branches move towards me, carrying bags of some sort. I scoot back away from them as they get nearer, swatting at one when it gets too close. Suddenly it's all too much, and the terror I have just gone through grips my consciousness. I yank the cover up over my face, trying to protect myself from all the unknowns around me.

"JADE, please don't be scared. Mystic is simply bringing in the items we acquired for you. I know this all has to be confusing, as the likeliness of you ever being around one such as Mystic or myself is rare for your kind. Mystic is asking for permission to talk to you. Neither of us want you to be scared and I fear we are pushing you too hard."

.   .   .

I DON'T SAY ANYTHING. I just rock back and forth grabbing the sides of my head, sinking further into my own mind. "Please, make it all go away. I don't want to hurt anymore. I don't want to fear all the unknowns. Please, just make it all stop." I must have been whispering the prayer aloud because something answers me back, but not out loud, in my head.

"LITTLE HUMAN, let your mind rest. You are safe within my arms and in time your prayers will be answered. Take this time to gather your strength, as everything has been provided for you. You can stop the fight to survive momentarily, as you will need your strength in the future."

SUDDENLY, a calmness enters my body, and I relax. I must have dozed off to sleep, only to awaken later to the sound of humming and the smell of food. Glancing around, the large guy has been turned over onto his back, but he still hasn't moved.

THE GHOST GIRL pops in front of me so quickly I screech. "Sorry, I forget sometimes that others are not used to me just appearing. You look less frazzled, Jade, the rest must've helped to clear your mind some. Mystic sorted through the bags Katherine sent and she has placed some food on a table near the back if you feel like eating. Once your belly is full, you can go through the clothing and pick out something you favor."

"WHAT ABOUT HIM?"

SHE GLANCES BACK at the guy, a frown on her face. "He is healing, but the burns worry me. As you can see, my form will not allow me to physically touch him and he needs medical attention. I'm at a loss on what to do. He will heal on his own, given enough time, but time will take a toll on his body's strength. If I leave to go acquire help, he will hate me. He would rather perish than be at the mercy of another. There seems to be no right answer where he is concerned that I can come up with. He ties me to this world, without him I too will perish."

"WHO IS HE? He was not happy to see me here. Should I leave before he regains consciousness?"

"EVEN THOUGH IT may not be obvious, he is my brother, and the feeling of happiness is not something I believe he has ever felt. He is in no position or even capable of hurting you at this time, so no you don't need to leave. Mystic granted you safe haven just as she did him all those rotations ago. You will always be welcome within her arms. If he proves to be a problem, she will handle it. Even with his renowned strength, he won't go against her wishes."

She motions towards a raised area. "Come, let's get some food in you." Gritting my teeth, I manage to rise. Turning slightly away from her, I pull the covering away, not shocked to see the amount of bruising covering my entire side or the blood that has dried on my legs and feet from all the cuts I have obtained.

Faltering, I push forward, practically falling against the table as my feet pulse in pain. Getting as close as I can, I grab the first thing I see. Shoving it into my mouth, not taking the time to actually taste anything before forcing my dried throat to swallow. When I start choking, I make myself slow down, not willing to get sick, and end up throwing it all back up. My eyes get big when I see a small limb lift what appears to be a jug of clear liquid up and sit in front of me.

Reluctantly, I reach forward and with weak fingers manage to screw the top off. I end up dumping half of it on me, as it seems I have forgotten how to take a drink. The cool liquid tastes unlike anything I have ever tasted before, and immediately, I feel my body absorbing it like some sort of rare nectar.

After drinking my fill, I make myself slow down and enjoy each bite as food has become a luxury … I think. Overly full, I make myself stop. When I see what's left, I begin looking for a place to hide the rest of it. I jump when I hear my name.

"Jade, you don't have to put any of that away or hide it. There is plenty where that comes from, and more will be brought to you each rotation. I know it will take time to prove that my words are true, but please take them to heart. I'm simply treating you the way I would hope another would me if I found myself in a new place all alone and scared.

"There is clothing and cleaning cloths in the other bag. Katherine also told me that she put something called a first aid kit in there as well. I personally don't know what that is, but I believe it is something that will ease your pain and make you heal quicker."

The prospect of being clean overrides the fear of all the unknowns around me. Somehow I know it's been a lengthy amount of time since anyone has been kind to me and the offer of clothing brings tears to my eyes. I tuck the covering around me suddenly aware of my nakedness underneath. Ellaria flickers a few times, and I see her beautiful face scrunch up like she is in pain.

. . .

"ARE YOU OK?"

"STRONG EMOTIONS bother me from time to time, but I'll be fine."

SCOOTING OVER, I grab the bag. Carefully, I pull the neatly rolled things out, one by one. Abruptly, I set it all away from me. Overwhelmed by the kindness that is being shown to me, a perfect stranger. No one gives you something for nothing.

"WHAT DO you want from me? I have no way of paying you for all of this."

SHE SMILES SADLY AT ME. "You don't owe me, nor any other, a single thing, Jade. Kindness is all I'm trying to show you, as I know you have had very little of it in quite some time. All I request is that you take the time to heal and rest your weary soul. One day you may have to do this for another.

"YOU HAVE no reason to trust me, and your fears are well earned. Your emotions are bombarding me, I can feel your pain as if it was my own. Between the two of you." She points to the male and then me. "I am weakening quickly. So, don't worry if I vanish for a while. I may have to leave you for a short span to clear my thoughts."

SHE SEEMS SO SINCERE, and she has done nothing so far to make me doubt her words. So I pull the bag back over, finding the first aid kit at the bottom with the cleaning cloths. Taking the rags out, I turn away again, heading towards a darker place back in the corner. Once I feel like I'm out of sight, I look back to make sure she isn't looking. She is hovering over the male, humming a tune that I have never heard before.

LETTING the cover drop to the floor, I painstakingly start wiping myself down, horrified at the scars and cuts that seem to line practically every inch of my skin. Some cuts are older and the skin has whitened, others are still red and puffy. I don't remember how I acquired any of these. At this point, I don't know if that's a good thing or a bad one. The rags end up black and dirty, in pieces by the time I get the majority of what I can off my battered body. However, I still feel like I smell of animal waste and wood smoke.

THERE ISN'T ENOUGH LEFT for me to do anything with my hair, so I finger comb what I can, then bundle it up in a loose, dirty bun. I could use a good hard scrubbing, but at least the majority of the dirt is gone. Pulling the first aid kit out, I look for a few bandages large enough to put on the bottom of my feet. That's when I notice the small device with a note on the top.

Hello, and welcome. I wish I was there to help you with this, but Ellaria said you needed some space. The little black machine does wonders for our human skin, simply place it on the wound. Then hit the two side buttons at the same time. It will feel funny, but once the lights turn green you should be healed, mostly. Use it anywhere needed. Please, don't hesitate to ask Ellaria for anything you might need. I'll try to send more stuff tomorrow.

Xoxo Katherine.

I don't know what is more shocking, the note itself or the fact that I can read it. It's like I know things about everything else, just not myself. Anytime I try, my head feels like it's going to explode. *What happened to me? Is someone out there looking for me right now? Do I have a family?* I hate this not knowing.

. . .

AT THIS POINT, I should just accept things as they are because the more I try to think about it, the more confused I become. No one does anything for another without some sort of gain for themselves. *What am I missing here?*

HESITANTLY, I put the small black box-like thing over a small scratch on my leg and hit the buttons, ready to jerk it back immediately if it starts to do more damage. I do feel it tingle slightly, but then the lights turn green and to my own amazement, the cut is healed. The mark is so small it probably won't even leave a scar. Not that it matters by the looks of the rest of me. My entire body seems to be riddled in marks, and that's just what I can see.

I USE the machine on my feet next and sigh in relief when I no longer have shooting, sharp pains going up my legs. The bottoms are still tender, but nothing like they were. I end up using it on everything I can see, tired of my body hurting all over.

A DEEP GROAN sounds loudly around us and I stop to glance back at the injured guy laying on the floor. Holding the machine up, I wonder if it would help him like it has me, but I don't really want to go near him again.

. . .

Setting the little healing box down, I start rummaging through the rest of the clothing. When I find a pair of panties, I immediately tug them on. They are loose on me, but they make me feel almost normal again. Then I grab a soft t-shirt and a pair of leggings that were rolled up together. To my surprise, there are several other outfits lining the bottom of the bag. I don't know that I have ever been more grateful to have real clothes on.

"I take it that you have found a few things to your liking?"

"Ellaria, I'm very thankful for all you have done for me. I feel so much better now. It's amazing the things we all take for granted until we no longer have them. Please excuse my actions before. Trust is not something that comes easily for me. Even though my thoughts and memories are foggy.."

"You have not been treated well, Jade. You have every right to be cautious. I have not taken your actions towards me as offensive at all. You are simply reacting as any other would in your place. I know things are confusing right now, but things will sort themselves out in time."

. . .

HOLDING up the black healing box. "Would you like to use this on him? I have no idea how it works, but it sure did a number on me."

"I CAN SEE FIRSTHAND it accelerated your healing. However, I can't use it on him."

"WHY NOT, won't it work on him?"

"I HAVE NO WAY OF KNOWING." She twirls around, holding her arms out. "As you can clearly see, there is nothing solid about me. From time to time, I can touch something and actually feel it beneath my palms, but nothing as dense as that box you are holding."

I STAND HERE with this thing in my hand leery. Do I step forward and try to help a guy that didn't want me here? Or do I step back and watch him suffer when I might have the means to help him? Ugh, why do I even ask myself these questions?

Chapter Six

Jade

Ellaria doesn't push me or even ask me to help. She simply floats there next to him, the love she feels for him apparent in her otherworldly eyes. He groans again, and I find myself beside him before I realize I have even moved. With the majority of my own wounds healed and some food in my belly. I almost feel normal if there is such a thing.

Gently, I move a piece of black ratted fabric off his chest. Closing my eyes for a second, as I have to swallow quickly to keep from throwing the food I just ate back up. Raw skin and blisters line the indentions of his side. Some of the larger ones have busted and are oozing a yellow type liquid out of them. I have never seen such burns, I can't imagine the pain he is in right now. When I try to move another piece of cloth off of him I find that it's stuck.

Ellaria floats on the other side of him, wringing her hands together nervously.

"From just what's visible, this is bad, Ellaria. Are you sure there is nowhere or no one who can come here to help him?" She shakes her head no. "Ok, then all we can do is our best. I know these clothes have got to come off, just how to do it though without hurting him worse, I'm not sure. Especially without water to loosen them up or something sharp to cut the material with."

"Jade, he is as alone in this world as you are. Even my presence is normally not wanted by him, but he tolerates me more than the others. SiN's mind has been poisoned by the ones who should have loved and cared for him."

"Did you just call him … SiN?"

. . .

"THAT IS what he has chosen to be called."

"WHAT MOTHER NAMES her child something like that?"

" A MONSTER. The moment he was old enough to understand its meaning she called him … Her SiN. She was nothing but a bitter woman who poisoned anything and everything she touched. Instead of him seeking out another way of life, he absorbed her cruelty and anger and became the exact thing he always said he didn't aspire to be … her. She lied to him about his birth and everything that followed and no matter how many others prove her words wrong, his path in his mind is set. A path that will destroy him one day if he doesn't see past his own hatred. I fear his constant denial and false blame are what's put him in his current condition. Time and time again I have wondered if things would have been different if I had made it, or if I would have been the same as he is now."

"I DON'T UNDERSTAND what happened to you or him, but right or wrong, no one should have to suffer like this. Is there a way to get some water up here? Or is it possible that you could go ask the girl who gave me all these supplies for a knife of some sort?"

· · ·

I just about climb out of my own skin when the voice of the tree surrounds us. "Jade, I apologize for startling you, but I can help maneuver him around enough that you can remove his clothing. He has some holding containers on the opposite wall. They may have what you require. As for water, I can provide a small reservoir of that as well.

Ellaria and I both move towards the containers I had not noticed before. Because they are the exact same shade as the surrounding walls, a person would simply walk past them unless they knew the containers were there. One of the lids opens up on its own. Peering into it, there are an array of things. From extra clothing to small chips that may be some form of currency. I even find another small black box like the one that was sent to me for healing, but its lights won't come on.

When we don't find a knife in that one, the other one opens. I gasp at the amount of weapons that line its floor. Even though I have no idea how to use any of these, there is no denying the amount of firepower he is stocking in here; it looks like he is preparing for a war.

"Oh my, was he planning on taking over a small county with all of this?"

. . .

"My brother doesn't need weapons. He is one all in himself, so these being here shock me."

Moving a few of the larger things around. I nick my finger on a blade hidden on the bottom. "Owww, damn it." I stick my finger in my mouth. "I'm tired of everything being out to hurt me." Shaking my hand, I pick up the huge, dagger-like knife. "This is a lot larger than what I am comfortable with, but it will have to do."

Reluctantly, I turn around, telling myself that if it were me lying there. I would hope some random stranger would try to help me out. When I start to lean back down at his side. I notice that a small pool of water has magically appeared in an indention on the floor. Getting back up, I reopen the bags that were brought here for me. Looking for anything I can use as a rag to wipe him down with. When I turn back, I'm alone.

"Ellaria?"

"I'm still here. I simply need a break. The entire forest is full of emotions right now and even though I'm trying, it's becoming overwhelming." I can hear her voice, but can't see her any longer. "Please proceed without me. I will return after I have regained some of my strength."

KNEELING BACK DOWN ALONE, I try to figure out where to start. He is a damn mess, should I start from the easiest to the hardest? His face appears to have the least amount of damage, with only a few minor burns close to his ears. Picking up the small black box, I click the buttons, only for the lights to turn yellow immediately.

NOT KNOWING WHAT THAT MEANS, I turn it back off and lay it down. Now what? *Maybe it won't work through all this dirt.* Wetting the cloth, I gently start wiping his face off. Starting on the undamaged side first, as he is covered in ashes and dust. Each swipe uncovers more of his unique features.

PALE GRAY SKIN is like soft velvet beneath my fingertips. Gently, I wipe the dust off his high cheekbones, admiring the long black eyelashes laying on them that most females would envy. A masculine chin accentuates pale pink lips. They are clenched tightly even in sleep, as his body fights off the pain and infection of these burns. He is beautiful in a terrifying way, even lying here trembling.

•   •   •

IT TAKES me a minute to realize one of the biggest differences between his face and other guys'. He has no facial hair. The area where his eyebrows would normally be is simply darker, like a natural outline of the bright yellow orbs that are once again staring up at me.

I DON'T MAKE a move as the last time he looked at me I fell out of the tree. His unfocused eyes search my face. He whispers a word that takes me a moment to understand. "Angel." Then closes his eyes back.

"I HAVE BEEN CALLED a lot of things, my new gray friend, but Angel was never one of them … I think."

HIS BODY RELAXES some and I start back where I left off, aggravated that the little black box still is not working on him. His neck has a few deep burns on it, but the top of this cloak seems to have blocked certain places on his skin better than others. The ends of his long black hair has also been singed, but I will deal with that at a later time.

AFTER A FEW MINUTES, I decide to get as much of this fabric off his skin as possible, then work on cleaning him the rest of the way up. His skin needs to breathe to heal, and this is taking too long like this. Soaking the pieces that are stuck, it seems like it takes me forever to get the cape off the upper part of his shoulders. Thankfully, there was no material on his chest, but if there had been, it may have kept him from getting so badly burned there.

MYSTIC HAS BEEN SKILLFULLY TURNING his large frame one way, then another. Almost like she knows my inner thoughts and what I need from her before I can say it. But I reckon if she can talk to me in my head. My thoughts should be just as easy.

WHEN I REACH for his pants, I almost turn away. I know how I felt waking up naked, but his pants are riddled and peppered with holes. A couple of really bad burns on his hip makes the final decision for me. Slowly, I start cutting the pants away, making sure to take my time and not nick him with this gigantic knife. Unfortunately, I have received several more cuts myself on as I keep trying to figure out how to hold it. The material around his waistline I have to soak. So while I'm waiting, I try to tackle the boots on his feet. "Mystic, do you have any idea how to get these off?"

TWO SMALL LIMBS curl around me. They click buttons I had not noticed and skillfully maneuver the massive boot things off. Then they pull what appears to be slender socks off his very human-looking feet once they move away. Well, if a size seventeen plus is normal. He is so large lying here on the floor. I can't imagine how big he is standing up. Hopefully, I will be long gone before he is up running around. Just ain't quite sure where I will go. I push that harrowing thought away, refocusing on him.

ONCE HE IS COMPLETELY NAKED, it's hard to ignore the elephant in the room. I constantly shift my eyes everywhere beside the thing that is blatantly staring me in the face. At one point, I throw the towel over it so that I can move it over without actually touching it, as it lays limply on his thigh. Apparently, the things they say about guys with big feet are true, because … this very manly thing is worth admiring. Even a blind woman wouldn't be able to miss the differences between a human male and well whatever he is.

THE RAG IS BLACK, and at this point, I'm not sure if I am just pushing dirt from one aspect of his body to the next.

"MYSTIC, we need some type of burn cream, and a way to dry these blisters up. I know I was never a nurse. He is just laying here waiting to get an infection or worse with these wounds open. If not treated, these burns on his side are going to scar terribly."

"I WILL SEE if any of the other Guardians can help with a soothing cream."

SHE NO LONGER SAYS THIS than an odd, squeaky voice sounds from below. "Mystic, hello … are you there?"

"I HAVE AWAKENED MOSSY OAK."

"OH, thank the stars. I come myself because the ones closest to you weren't sure if you were still slumbering or not. I hate to visit with bad news, but I come with a message: we have to move. SAGE just sent out a warning to all in the entire dark forest. Solanar apparently is falling and they are projecting it to crash right into our territory within half a rising. I have already told the smaller saplings to start moving past our normal perimeter. Those youngsters gave me a hard time until I threatened to tell you."

THERE IS no missing the terror in the voice echoing around me. Getting to my feet, I walk hesitantly to the edge of the opening, and peer out. I don't know who is more shocked. The very tall pine-like tree with a face looking up, or me seeing a face within the limbs of the tree.

"The tree is talking," I whisper out.

I swear I hear laughter inside my mind, right before Mystic speaks up. "Don't think about it too hard, Jade. This is Mossy Oak, she is a dear friend."

"But ... she is a tree."

"So, am I."

Oookkkayyy. This is freaky. I wave slowly down at the pretty tree below and can't help but laugh when one of her small limbs waves back.

"Mystic, I didn't know you had company. Welcome."

.   .   .

"Mossy Oak, this is Jade. If things are as dire as you say. I need to find a way to protect my organics further. Mossy Oak, did SAGE say how this came to be?"

"All SAGE said was that a bomb had gone off, and it damaged SCOUT somehow, knocking him offline, and now Solanar is not responding. She is hopeful they can get it fixed quickly, but she still wants us to get out from under its orbit. Mystic, I am concerned, do you still have the ability to uproot? I know it's been Orbital rotations since you've moved, but there is no missing the platform will hit either here or close by. You are the oldest of us, we can't lose your guidance in these trying times."

"My roots have sunk too deeply into the very core of Darverius, and I can no longer remove myself from this location. Thank you, Mossy Oak, for coming to warn me personally, but you are to never put yourself in direct danger for me again. If you can't connect with me through our root system, then take matters into your own limbs. No one life is more important than another's."

"Mystic, I simply can't bear the thought of you being crushed under the massive weight of that platform. Now that

I know you can't move, do you think if we all gathered close to you, we could support it together?"

"No, my sweet sapling. My base and limb reach are still higher than most. There is no reason to sacrifice any others. We will leave this to the Lord of Light, be his will I'll survive this. Now be on your way, and if you see Ellaria within the forest, tell her I need her assistance quickly, as Jade will need to be moved to a safer location. You go on, the young ones will need your assurances and guidance."

I watch in amazement as the pine-like tree walks away on its roots and in the distance. It looks like the entire forest is uprooting and moving away.

"Mystic, how are we going to move him?"

"There is nowhere safe for him to go, so he will remain with me. Unlike you, there are several in the area I would trust with your welfare. All I ask of you is that you don't inform them that he is here within me. I know the boy has his faults, and he just keeps doing things I don't approve of. However, deep down, I know he is better than his choices. His heart has not been shown another path. A youngling should be taught love and nurturing by its mother. He was never given that care and is simply reacting because he knows no other way. SiN chooses to remain on a path that will destroy him one rising. I have tried to reason with him, but he has to decide to change on his own. Not for the sake of others."

"Is this why you have sheltered him all this time?"

"Yes, and no. He came to me lost, searching as a youngling for the one he is still convinced did his mother wrong. At first, I could not see past the darkness that resides in him and I refused him shelter. Then one rose I saw a glimpse of what he could be and I have held him close, keeping his secrets since. In his heart, I'm all he has, and I will not turn him away. Nor allow him to be harmed while in my grasp."

"So he also turns from Ellaria?"

"Unfortunately yes, and until recently, he was unaware of her existence. She has been with me much longer than he and even though I knew of their connection, it was not my story to tell. Anger does nothing but poison the soul, and he is full of it."

. . .

"I'm sorry, Mystic, to have added to your burden, I thank you for taking me in even if it's just for a short time. What can I do to help you? What is this Solanar?"

"Solanar is a floating city, at one time it was the primary defense system that protected Darverius. There is nothing you can do besides what you already are, you are not responsible, nor can you stop future events. Tend to him the best you can and pray, child, because we are going to need all the help we can get."

She goes quiet, and I swear I can feel the entire tree flexing and moving beneath my feet. Frustrated and helpless, I go back to my patient who, if possible, looks worse with each passing minute. "Mystic, is he dying? Shouldn't he have awakened by now even in this condition?"

"I gave him a strong sedative when he first arrived. Your organic bodies don't heal well under the duress of pain. I thought it would give him a fighting chance; now that decision may bury us together here forever if I can't withstand the weight of Solanar. At least he won't be awake to feel anything. Jade, you should go ahead and prepare to leave, or you may become trapped in here yourself. Things are quickly deteriorating and Solanar is falling slightly quicker than the others anticipated."

"Do you really believe I would be safer out there than in here with you?"

"The chances of you making it out of range before Solanar falls is slim, whether you stay or go."

Choking up, I just nod yes before wringing out the rag once again. I might as well stay busy, dwelling on the things I can't change never helps. A single tear runs down my cheek landing lightly upon the skin on his chest as I lean over him, and I swear it looked like he jerked.

Chapter Seven

Jade

I DON'T KNOW how much time passes, but the sound of a loud screeching noise surrounding us jerks me out of my own thoughts. "Mystic?"

"BRACE YOURSELF."

THAT'S ALL the warning I get before the sky darkens and the very air around me becomes pressurized. I scream out when the floor beneath my knees buckles and we both end up rolling towards the center of the hollowed out opening of Mystic's sanctuary.

I GRAB ONTO HIM, draping myself over his body protectively as the sound of breaking limbs and pieces of bark rain down upon us. The walls inside this chamber begin to buckle and I close my eyes, hugging the massive body beneath me tighter.

JUST WHEN I think Mystic is about to buckle underneath the weight pushing down upon her, Ellaria appears out of nowhere, pressing herself against the main interior wall. Her hands sink deeply within the grooves and cracks that have just formed.

A GLOW unlike anything I have ever seen before envelops the area around us. Mystic's entire base lights up to the point I can see the veins that run the nutrients up and down her massive trunk. I hear them both screaming in my mind and then what sounds like a jet engine roars to life.

ELLARIA STARTS to flicker like a strobe light, her body going in and out of focus so fast my eyes can't keep track. The pressure inside the room begins to fade and I watch in amazement as Mystic's trunk starts to straighten back up.

· · ·

ELLARIA REMOVES her hands from the wall and floats unsteadily towards us, if that's even possible. The closer she comes the lighter she appears. She falls to her knees and touches her brother tenderly before looking over at me.

"YOU ARE the light that can heal him, please save my brother."

BEFORE I CAN QUESTION her words. Her eyes roll back in her head, and she mist away like particles in the wind. An anguished howl echoes throughout the forest, followed by several more. I have no idea what just happened, but I know it's bad.

THE ROOM DIMS and I glance down at the male I have been holding close to me. He is still unresponsive, and I'm not sure if that is good or bad. "Mystic, are you ok? What just happened?"

THE SADNESS that suddenly fills my mind makes me sob as Mystics' feelings overwhelm me. Then she whispers, "Ellaria just sacrificed her very life's essence to save … us. She infused my core with the last of her strength. She is now lost to us, in the in-between. As for me. I will heal in time. We owe her everything as the weight of Solanar was too extreme for me to hold alone."

I FEEL MYSTIC PULL AWAY, and the tree trembles and shakes all around me as she settles her large upper limbs back into place. Looking down, my first thoughts are. *Would he have done that for her if the tables had been turned? I only knew Ellaria for a short time, but she made me believe … there was more than evil in this world. Is she really gone, or was she ever here?*

SUDDENLY WEARY. I lay my head down upon his chest, comforted by the beating of his heart and the steady movement of his breathing. The sounds of the grieving howls outside tear at my heart as I cry myself to sleep.

KATHERINE

We all gather next to the shuttle, watching in horror as Solanar comes closer and closer. When suddenly, I am knocked to my knees screaming out. I grab my head as Thorns' grief completely overwhelms my mind.

. . .

VOICES SURROUND me right before muscular arms lift me up off the ground as I fight past Thorns' emotions. A vision of Ellaria enters my mind, and that's when I know something horrible has happened to her.

I REACH for her spirit only to be forced back by a darkness that has me screaming out in terror. Somehow Ellaria's spirit has been taken by mistake and she is now being judged for the sins of her brother. I can hear her screams of torment and feel the skin being torn from her bones.

HEEDLESS of myself or the consequences. I push past her pain and appear within a realm I hoped to never return, placing myself between Ellaria and the entity that is torturing her unjustly, The Keeper of Souls.

"STOP THIS MADNESS. Leave her be and let her pass into the light. You are judging the wrong soul for its trespasses; she is innocent!" I scream out to the unknown entity around me.

A BOOMING VOICE echoes all around. "Sweet Katherine, I wondered what it would take for you to step back into the in-between. I have missed you; I so love the taste of your fear on my tongue. Your parents' souls released you from this realm, why do you return now, knowing that there is the possibility you will be trapped here with me forever?"

"Ellaria does not deserve to be punished, she is good and pure, you know this. She has barely survived in the state you've allowed her to exist in since her birth. What sick pleasures do you get from treating her so?"

"Oh, my Katherine. I didn't do this for or to her. The sins of the mother were so extreme they were passed onto her children. You are the only one capable of righting a wrong that should have never occurred. If you are willing to take on this task, I will release her soul back to you to watch over until the time comes for her to exist as another. If you fail me on this task, I will take you both in payment to do with as I will."

"Is this task doable?"

"Depends on your sway of the others and your quick wits. Be assured this will not be an easy decision. I will not intervene again one way or another, nor give you a way out if you fail before her time has come to an end."

. . .

I LOOK BACK AT ELLARIA, not really seeing the image she has portrayed herself as, but as a spirit. Her inner glow grows dimmer the longer we stand here talking.

"WHAT DO YOU WANT FROM ME?"

"ARE you sure you should take this task on without discussing this with your mate? I need you to be clear on this, Katherine. My terms in allowing her soul to be released back to you are as stated. If you fail at this task. I will take you both in payment, have no doubt about this. My wrath will not be kind and your mate will feel your suffering for all of eternity, with no way to save or avenge you."

"I WILL NOT FAIL."

"HOLD OUT YOUR PALM."

I CAN'T STOP the whimper that leaves me as his mark burns its way onto my palm.

· · ·

"You have until the mark fades to fulfill this task. If it disappears before you are taken, you will know that you satisfied my terms."

"What do you require from me?"

"What was once whole was shattered. A single soul split in two that needs to be made as one. The initial sin must be atoned for … For where there is death, there will always be death. The moment one life force is given to save another, her soul must be transferred into one that has not formed. If this happens, both intertwined souls will be forgiven. Now be gone before I change my mind."

Chapter Eight

Jade

WITH ARMS SWINGING WILDLY and Ellaria's name on his lips. I'm thrown halfway across the hollowed-out room. One of Mystic's small limbs catches me right before I hit the wall hard.

THRASHING AROUND, SiN screams out Ellaria's name over and over. Scrambling to my feet. I run back to him, trying my best to stop him from injuring himself worse, but he tosses me around like I weigh nothing.

. . .

"Noooooo, stop hurting her." His body curves up unnaturally as a tortured scream leaves his lips.

"Mystic, help me," I scream.

Small limbs come out of the floor, wrapping themselves around the uninjured areas of his body. He strains against them, cutting himself more in the process. Sobbing now, he just keeps whispering her name and the absolute agony in his voice brings forth my own tears.

I grab his head, tucking it into my chest, then place my hand above his heart, rocking him back and forth. Humming the song she had sang to him earlier. Trying anything to get him to stop fighting the restraints.

It feels like forever before he finally calms down. His entire body collapsing like a dead weight in my arms. Horrified that this fit has made him turn for the worst. I move my hand away, replacing it with my head so that I can make sure he still has a heartbeat. I'm grateful it's beating so hard it's moving my entire head. That is when I notice the blood on his chest.

. . .

"Dammit, he is bleeding again. Mystic, I think he is back out. You can let go of him now, but don't go too far in case he takes another fit." I grab the rag, immediately throwing it down with a hiss when I see the deep cut on the palm of my hand.

Holding the cut closed the best I can, I rummage around the first aid kit I had never put up looking for some gauze to wrap around it. No band-aid will stay on this spot and the only other rag I have available was used to clean him up.

Finally, finding something I could use, I wrap it around my palm tightly. The whole time, never taking my eyes off him. Once I've covered it the best I can, I scoot back over to him. Picking the rag up I had used earlier on him with my other hand.

Gently, I start wiping my blood off his burns only to stop dead in my tracks. The burns are gone.... I lay my hand back down just inches from touching his skin not believing my eyes.

A perfectly healed hand print is now in the place where his burns were only moments ago. The rest of his skin all around it is still in the same horrible condition it was. I watch as water dripping from the rag mixes with my blood that still remains and the moment my blood touches the burns they start to heal.

Backing away, I close my eyes and shake my head. "Ok, your eyes are messing with you, Jade, because of all the stress you have been through. This is all in your mind. He simply didn't have any burns in that area, and you are imagining this."

But when I look back down at the handprint, it's still there. Unwrapping my hand, I take my finger and cover it with some of the blood that is still in my palm. Hesitantly, I touch a place on the side of his neck with it. He trembles, slightly moaning out as the wound completely closes right before my eyes. His skin sucks in my blood like it's a miracle drug.

Jumping to my feet I back away from him as far as I can. "Mystic, something freaky is going on here. Are you seeing this?"

"I am."

"What should I do?"

. . .

"IT's NOT my life force, any decision regarding so comes from you."

I can see him shivering and twitching all over as the worst of the blisters seep down his side. His face is scrunched up in pain and for some reason, all I keep hearing are Ellaria's words. "*Save my brother.*" Taking a deep breath, I step back towards him.

"MYSTIC, will you keep him under until I'm finished? I really don't want him to wake up until this is over and I'm out of the way."

"HE WILL REMAIN AS HE IS."

"OK, here goes, you can do this. First thing, Jade, stop talking to yourself. Humans have spare blood; they donate it all the time; this is no different. You are just going to smear it on the worst places and then well I don't know what will happen, but you can't leave him to suffer like this. There has to be a logical explanation and where your memory is messed up, you just can't remember what it is."

. . .

I KNEEL down next to him. Squeezing the cut on my palm, waiting until a few fresh lines of blood appear before lowering it to his skin. Gently, I rub my hand all over his side, making sure the worst of the burns are covered completely. My hand is starting to sting like fire, but I have to finish this before I chicken out. Taking my finger, I dab the places on his neck and face. Already, I can see the burns getting smaller. I lather the worst burn on his hip twice as it seems to be the deepest and step back slightly light-headed. I have no idea how much of my blood I have smeared on him, but it looks like a murder scene.

GRASPING MY PALM TIGHTLY, I re-wrap it. I have done all I can, even if this has felt entirely wrong. Looking down, there is dried blood and skin from his burns on my legs where I was leaning over him earlier. My clothes are saturated with the liquid that his skin was pushing out and my hair is full of dust from earlier. I feel nasty all over and there are no cleaning rags left.

"MYSTIC, in the aftermath of all that's happened, I hate to ask this, but is there any place I can wash off?"

"THE ENTIRE AREA is vacant right now of all activity. It should be safe for you to bathe in a nearby stream. Once you are ready to leave, I will lower you down to the surface and show you the path."

"WILL you still be able to see me?"

"YES, I can actually see all of the forest one way or another. Because of our bond, you will be able to call out for me no matter where you are in the forest, and I will know it."

THE NEED TO be out of this hole and away from him has me practically running to the bag that has the other pieces of clothing in it. Grabbing the first thing I see; I make my way to the opening. I don't bother looking down at him again. All of a sudden, I find myself overwhelmed by everything that has occurred and my involvement in it. I need some time alone to gather my thoughts and figure out my next step. Because I know the moment he awakens, things will change drastically.

A SMALL OPENING appears in front of me along with a huge limb. I step out hesitantly, grasping onto a smaller twig that is hanging out. I can't seem to stop the squeal that leaves my lips when another limb wraps around my waist before the large one, I'm standing on turns midair lowering me all the way to the ground. Stepping off of it, I can't help but laugh, "That's the most fun I have had in ages." I yell up at Mystic.

A PATH PARTS right in front of me and without a second thought I start down it, amazed at the scenery around me. The last time I was on the forest floor I was terrified, hungry, and hurt. It's astonishing what a few days will do for a person's outlook on life.

THE STREAM APPEARS before I know it, and I hesitate when I notice the color. The water is not green, blue, or even clear. It has a milky white appearance. "Ugh, Mystic, can you hear me?"

I FEEL her nudge my mind. "Is this safe for me?"

WHAT FEELS like humor comes back to me and a small root lifts up from the ground, pushing me forward playfully.

"I WILL TAKE THAT AS A YES." Then I start talking to myself again. "Lord, you know there is gonna be some sort of creepy crawling nasty in there, but I have to get this funk off me."

. . .

PULLING off the soft-soled shoes I have on. I dip a toe quickly in the so-called water and back out. When nothing attacks me and my toe doesn't fall off, I take one last look around before stripping completely out of the clothes I have on.

WALKING IN, I am expecting the soil to feel slimy, but it feels oddly dry against the soles of my feet. I didn't know that was possible in water, but it's like I am on dry ground. The water has no smell at all and feels like silk running through my fingertips.

THERE IS a small rock setting about six inches under the water and I sit down on it, taking the time to enjoy this one moment where nothing is trying to hurt me, and my belly is full. From here, I can see a few broken limbs lying around and piles of fresh leaves that appear to have fallen before their time.

THESE MUST HAVE BEEN from Mystic when she was trying to hold up that city thing. I look up into the sky, but nothing is above us. Hopefully, they fixed it, and it won't come back this way again.

I BECOME SO ENGROSSED in getting clean I completely push the rest of the world and all the unknowns away. Giving my mind time to just mute. Even scrubbing my hair three times. I still feel dirty, but I have been in the water so long my hands are pruning up.

LOOKING DOWN at the cut on my hand, I'm shocked that the water has not hurt it worse than it has. The bleeding has stopped mostly now, and it's just slightly bruised where I was squeezing it to get more blood. Just thinking about what I did is messed up in so many ways. Who needs blood smeared on their skin like a miracle cream to heal? More than likely, my mind was simply messing with me and when I return, he will still be all burned up. Only now lathered in my blood, and I will have to wash him down all over again.

I TAKE a second before getting out of the water to wash the clothes I had on, and I was wringing them out when I felt it. Something is coming for me.

Chapter Nine

SiN

GASPING FOR BREATH I rise straight up, disoriented, and confused. "Ellaria, Mystic?"

"I'M HERE, SiN."

GRABBING MY HEAD, I try to sort through how I got here. My skin is tingling all over and my chest feels heavy like I just lost something dear to me. "Ellaria!" I scream her name out and jump to my feet. Unsteady, I sway slightly, as I lean against the familiar walls of my sanctuary.

. . .

"Mystic, what has happened to me?"

"Do you not remember what you have done?"

"Yes, and no. I'm not sure how I got here. Wait, there … was an intruder, I saw her. Where is she now? How could you allow another in here?"

"Is that all you recall?"

My side is tingling and feels wet, then there is this smell that makes my mouth water and my gums hurt. My heart is beating so hard in my chest that it has me rubbing it absent-mindedly. Pulling my hand away quickly, I'm shocked when it comes away, covered in a substance I'm not sure I have seen before. I bring my hand up slowly to smell it, only for the scent to be so irresistible that I end up licking the blood from my palm.

Suddenly, I feel like I'm being tugged by an invisible string as I'm drawn to something outside my sanctuary. A smell, no, it's more than that, it's a pull unlike anything I have ever felt before. I start to mist away when Mystic closes the opening, stopping my escape. Panting, and desperate to see or feel what is just outside, I strike out, only for her to push me backwards, small limbs wrapping around my wrist when I try to force my way out.

"SɪN, you will calm yourself before you leave this place, or I will keep you trapped in here. I promised your sister I would protect that female and you will not have me going back on my word. I will not allow you to abuse Jade like you have the others who have tried to care for you. If you disobey me in this request, SiN, I will never welcome you here again. You will be banned from the Dark Forest all together; the moment you set foot within its boundaries the guardians will respond. Your behavior has become quite appalling, and after your sister's sacrifice to save you. I will no longer tolerate your disobedience."

"Wʜᴀᴛ sᴀᴄʀɪꜰɪᴄᴇ?" I no sooner say that, then Mystic shows me. Pictures, images, and feelings pulse through our bond. I can see the other guardians running away and feel Mystic's pain as the structure I caused to fall. Crashes into her, but that's not the worst of it. I watch in horror as Ellaria stands over me and another that I can't see clearly. Using her own strength to hold Mystic up until Solanar's thrusters reengaged. Thrusters that were offline because of the bomb I set off.

I HIT my knees screaming out her name, searching through the link that has always tied her to me even when I denied it. In an effort to spare her from the same shadows that plagued my soul, I refused to acknowledge her presence. I always knew she was there, watching in the mist.

FROM THE TIME we were younglings, I would catch a glimpse of her hiding, always watching … seeing the horrors around her … us, but not the capability to intervene. Even though we didn't speak I could always feel when she was around. She became a comfort in the loneliness that surrounded me until one rising, she too was gone.

ROTATIONS HAD PASSED since I had last felt her presence. I didn't even recognize the familiar bond when she first appeared before me. Screaming Ellaria's name once again, I slam my fist against Mystic's unforgiving wall, basting in the pain of my knuckles splitting open under the force.

NEVER IN A MILLION rotations could I have dreamed up the consequences of the bomb I set to destroy my brothers … the chosen ones. I was simply trying to find a way to save myself if things went wrong. In the end, all I did was destroy the one person who cared for me, even when she shouldn't have. Not only is Mystic showing me what happened while I lay helpless on the floor. I can feel Ellaria's last words as if I was standing above looking down. *You are the light that can heal him, please save my brother.*

WHAT HAVE I DONE? I can't think straight. It's this pull, it's messing with my head. Whoever has done this to me has tricked the others into believing they are good. My enemies must have sent this mystery female and because of her pres-ence here my sister is now gone. It's this female's fault that Ellaria was even in the area at all, and she will pay for taking my sister's life.

"MYSTIC, you have been deceived; release me at once!"

"YOU FOOLISH BOY! Mark my words, you will regret the actions of your past and your present if you don't look past the darkness that has consumed your soul."

"RELEASE ME, I have a sister to avenge."

. . .

SHE OPENS the door to the only home I have ever known. The moment I mist out of it, I know things will not be as they were for us, unless I can prove to her I am right.

I STREAK through the forest being pulled towards an unknown entity. In what feels like seconds, I emerge in a clearing next to one of the many small steams I have bathed in many times. Standing in the middle of the stream is a small human female. I look around, this can't be right. There is no way I am being drawn to something as inferior and weak as what stands before me scared and scrawny.

HER PALE SKIN is lined in whip marks, some still red, while older ones have turned to scars. Hair black as night, brushes along slim hips as she bends over, gathering water in her hands. Every rib can be counted on her sides, and I wonder how something so frail could have withstood the markings now covering her body.

TAKING A DEEP BREATH, her scent floods my system. I grasp my jaw as my gums feel like they are suddenly splitting apart. Running my tongue along my teeth, I'm instantly cut by a sharp, new incisor. Somehow, I now have fangs, and the urge to sink them deep into the slender neck standing clueless in front of me is almost overwhelming.

.   .   .

"WHAT SORCERY IS THIS? What have you done to make me crave something as repulsive as you?"

SHE SCREAMS, turning around so fast she falls back into the water. I'm upon her before she can make her next move. Grabbing her by the throat, I lift her straight up into the air. Her small hands fight against my hold as my hand starts to crush her windpipe.

HER FEAR SEEMS to awaken the unknown beast inside of me. Bringing her closer, I lick the tears that now run freely down her cheek as she kicks and squirms in my arms, trying to free herself.

"PLEASE."

THE SOUND of her voice makes me hesitate for some reason and I lower her to the ground but keep her within my clasp. "What have you done to me?" She shakes her head no, but I'm not falling for her act like the others did.

.   .   .

"Who sent you? How did you find my sanctuary? How did you lure Ellaria to you? You might as well answer me, female, there is no use in trying to protect whoever sent you. You will all pay a heavy price for my sister's life."

"Nobody sent me. I don't even know how I got here. Ellaria was the one who found me. I was hiding, and she just showed up, I swear."

"You lie! You were sent here to spy on me. They should have known I would see through this act of yours. They could have at least thrown one at me that was favorable to the eyes. Instead of sending a scarred and weak specimen like yourself. For future reference, you need to inform your employers I like my females with some meat on their bones. Did they really think I wouldn't suspect you because you're frail? I could easily break you in half."

Unexpectedly, her palm struck me right across the face, and I couldn't fathom where the fire inside of her came from.

"I should have let you die!"

. . .

I CAN'T HELP but laugh, "Just now realizing your mistake, are you? Stop evading the questions before I have to get more creative on how to get the answers. Who sent you?" I shake her hard and instead of her fighting back, she sighs wearily.

"IT DOESN'T MATTER what I say. You will never believe me anyway, but if I'm so repulsive why are you holding me so?"

SHE GOES limp in my arms and that makes me glance down. My arm is clutched around her waist, holding her naked skin up against mine. The sight of her small hand lying on my chest looks like it belongs there. Where her skin is wet, there are now streams of what appears to be a bright red liquid running down my naked chest and legs. My shaft hardens to my own disgust, and I throw her onto the bank just out of reach.

DUCKING MYSELF INTO THE WATER. I wash away whatever this disgusting liquid is covering my body. Noticing immediately that there isn't a single mark left upon my skin. *Were my injuries not as severe as I originally thought, or is the red liquid flowing through her veins what healed me?*

. . .

She is trying to scramble away when I appear in front of her again. She screams out Mystic's name, and this enrages me even more.

"Stop calling out for her, you don't deserve her assistance. Because of you, she has turned against me, and my sister is dead. I believe I will enjoy tearing you into small pieces just to see how loud you can scream."

She holds her hand out, like that is going to stop me, and keeps shaking her head no. All this movement does is heighten my knowledge of the veins pulsing right under her skin. With no knowledge of what I'm about to do. I yank her back against me and my new fangs sink deeply into the side of her neck. While I drink her life force, I grind myself against her soft mound, seeking the ultimate satisfaction only a female can provide.

My mouth has no longer filled with the absolute ambrosia of her blood when something hard twirls between us and she is ripped from my arms. I growl out, determined to destroy whoever took her from me only to find her being held by a small root. Red streaks roll down her pale skin, teasing my senses as it flows past her perky breast. That's when I realize it is the exact substance that had been applied to my body. She is the cause of this sudden hunger I can't seem to control.

"CLEVER GIRL, you thought that if you could make me hunger for you that you could control me. I'm sure you are disappointed that your hold on me is not as strong as you hoped for. The ones that sent you are wiser than I originally gave them credit. Not that this information will help you or them in the end."

I CIRCLE AROUND HER, Mystic intervening has given me a moment to clear my head of this hunger, but it only opens up more questions. Shaking, I notice she is holding her hand against the puncture holes I have put on her neck.

"YOU NEED NOT WORRY about those two little marks. They are the first of many scars I plan on adding to your skin. That is, if I can find a spot free to mark as my own."

MY HARSH WORDS make her flinch, and she tries in vain to cover herself. "You're a monster."

. . .

"THANK YOU FOR THE COMPLIMENT, flattery will get you nowhere."

SHE WATCHES me wearily from down-cast eyes, a howl echoing around us has her glancing away. That's when I notice the mark on her cheek. For some reason, the very thought of anyone marking her face besides myself, enrages me and I roar out in anger. This single mark brings out my inner beast as my mind sees the marks on her body with fresh eyes. Was she tortured and made to come here, are her words true?

SCRAMBLING BACK, she breaks away from the limb holding her and turns to run. I'm shocked at the laughter that now leaves me, as this is the very last thing she should have ever done. She apparently isn't aware that the path she is running along is going to quickly put her out of reach of any assistance she might have gotten from the guardians surrounding us.

I RE-CLOTHE myself with a simple thought and mist through the forest like a dark ghost chasing after a light. She stumbles a few times when she looks back to see if I'm following her. Unless I make myself known, she won't discover my presence until it's too late. She is so focused on me she doesn't see the other dangers getting ready to devour her as the Selin gather in on her from the sides.

. . .

STAYING CLOSE, I enjoy the sound of her heart pushing the blood through her veins. I wonder how she is going to react when she finally sees what is stalking her other than myself. Will she turn to me for assistance or fight until they eat her alive?

THE SECOND THAT thought hits me, I know I will never allow them or another to harm her, that privilege is mine solely. I grab her just as a large paw swipes at the location she was in. A terrified scream leaves her when she sees a jaw full of teeth snap right in front of her face seconds before I mist us both to a safer location.

I HAVE UNANSWERED QUESTIONS, and she is going to answer them. If they are not to suit me, then maybe we will play this game again. However, next time I will let the Selin play with her before rescuing her.

WITH A SINGLE THOUGHT, I land us just inside the dark forest, but close to my shuttle in case I need to leave in a hurry. I barely manage to throw her to the ground before she starts dry heaving. This is her body's way of handling misting for the first time, the few I have ever relocated this way always react similarly.

THE SIGHT of her curled up on the ground sick bothers me more than it should. I don't know who is more shocked, me or her, when I find myself leaning over her, pulling her long dark hair back away from her face. I become so distracted with the feeling of the dark, thick strands in my hands that when she tries to pull away, I growl down at her.

AGGRAVATED BY MY SUDDEN WEAKNESS, I grab her arm, pulling her upright to my face, snarling. Dark violet eyes stare back at me as she trembles in my arms. Her smell completely engulfs my senses, but there is something else I'm sensing. Fear is apparent, but it's the wonder in her eyes as she looks up at me that freezes this moment in time. I have never had one look past my appearance to the male inside, and I feel like she is peering into my soul. I don't move when she raises her hand, brushing a stray lock of my hair off my face.

"HOW COULD something so beautiful be so cruel? What did they do to make you so distrustful?"

. . .

For a second, I wonder if I have misjudged her. My arms wrap around her on their own, tucking her snuggly into my chest. I have no knowledge of how to comfort another and this goes against everything I am, so why do I crave her sudden approval? She has bewitched me. There is no other answer for this.

She has my emotions all over the place, and I dislike this sudden need for her greatly. It's like I can feel her underneath my skin, we are no longer two individuals but joined as one. Why did I just pull her close like a lover would and why isn't she pushing me away? Because of these thoughts, I am preoccupied and don't hear them, until it is too late.

Chapter Ten

SiN

QUICKLY WE ARE SURROUNDED. "Well, isn't this cozy, men! Who knew he had a soft spot for anyone? Keeping one for yourself, SiN? You know that's against the boss's rules. You owe us, and I'm thinking that little female in your arms will put a slight dent in your debts. So save us all some trouble and go ahead and send her over."

MY MIND immediately starts looking for an escape route, at least for the female. There is no way I can fight the sheer number of them closing in on us in this clearing. Their leader holds a laser Phaser-up and even though I could mist past him swiftly, it takes me longer to dissolve into the mist if holding someone else. The shot would go right through me, but the female would be vulnerable. He could easily kill her while I held her in my arms.

"Qyinn, I know our last meeting didn't work out in your favor, nor mine, but I will find a replacement for the female you were supposed to receive. Personally, I am shocked to see you here. I thought you never left your main ship." I pull the female behind me slowly, grateful she has enough sense to realize the danger around us. Her small hands grasp my cloak as she pushes herself up against my back. I lay a hand on her hip to keep track of her exact position behind me.

The Jynrel pirate looks around at his men and cackles out laughing. "I wanted to oversee your capture myself! SiN, your words of promise mean nothing to my superiors any longer. I was told to bring a female or your head. Right now, I'm willing to take both as a bonus."

In an attempt to discourage him from taking her. I grab the female roughly from behind me. "Look, she is puny and won't hold up like the other one would have. This one is even disfigured and ignorant. What you saw was me holding her up, as she is too weak to stand on her own." I throw her to the ground, hoping she will stay there. When I hear her gasp out in pain, I force myself to look away.

HE STARTS pacing in front of us, his eyes never leaving the female on the ground beside me. I step in front of her, blocking his view, trying to keep his focus on me.

"OH, is that what we saw, SiN? Because I could have sworn I witnessed some tenderness in the moments we have been observing you."

"YOU WERE OBVIOUSLY MISTAKEN. How did you find me?"

"OH, you may be a clever son of DaR, but we are not called pirates for nothing. Your shuttle was seen landing on Targres Four and even though we could not find it by sight alone, we have many devices that can see through any cloaking device. Once located, it was a simple matter to attach a homing beacon. We're thankful you weren't as injured as our sources had implied. We had prepared for an extended stakeout. You can only imagine our surprise when you casually walked towards us without a care in the world. Now you can either come along on your own, or we will make you. I long for you to take the second option."

. . .

THE SOUND of footsteps and the beating of wings has me turning away from the threat in front of me momentarily. As I reach down to grab the girl, a large figure lands right before me. I snarl when I see the smile on his perfect face. "Well RaZ, what do we owe the pleasure dear brother, were you worried about me?"

"YOU WISH."

HE LOOKS AROUND, flashing his large fangs at the pirates who have gathered closer since his arrival. My hand involuntarily reaches up to my mouth realizing the similarity I now have with the male in front of me. "Looks like I got here just in time for you to introduce me to your friends." He turns back towards me, his eyes immediately homing in on the female in my arms. His eyes flash a bright silver and his wings rustle aggressively as he gets right in my personal space. "You worthless whoremonger, you don't deserve to breathe another breath." He reaches out for her, and I step back, holding her just out of his grasp.

GLANCING DOWN AT HER, I will admit she does appear rough. Her hair is hanging in tangles, dirt covers her bare feet, and scratches marred the tender skin on her legs. She looks up at me with those dark violet eyes of hers, then around the clearing. The hopelessness in her expression bothers me the most, it's obvious she is overwhelmed. The fresh bite mark I had made on her neck is still bleeding slightly, the tender skin all around it is bruised. I can tell she is shutting down her emotions, simply willing herself to be somewhere else. This has become overwhelming to a mind that seems already fractured.

WHEN HE STARTS to reach for her again, I react, pressing her close to me, snarling at him like a rabid canine. Instinctively, she starts squirming against me, fighting the hold I have on her. Until another voice echoes throughout the clearing and she goes eerily still. Her eyes lift up to mine and then back towards the two males who just walked out of the forest. Her eyes focus upon the male I hate for the role he played in my creation, and I know she makes the connection of who he is to me by sight alone.

"PUT THE FEMALE DOWN, SiN. You have hurt enough people, son. It's time for you to stop this reign of terror."

THE VERY IDEA of him and the others being here enrages me. My body pulses with anger and I swear I feel myself getting larger as I pull the shadows in around us feeding off the darkness that created them. The small hand squeezing my arm is the only thing that keeps me from foolishly attacking the threats around us.

I HAD ALMOST FORGOTTEN about Qyinn and his men with the arrival of my father and brothers until he yells out, "Look, pack mates! It appears we come just at the right time. We are about to witness a family reunion. Commander, we didn't expect such a welcome party."

I HAVE to say when Father speaks up, it is quite intimidating. "Qyinn, you and your men have made an unauthorized landing on my planet, and I will not tolerate that type of disregard for the rules on my land. Take your men and leave before things turn ugly and I have to take matters into my own hands. I will not ask you again."

QYINN'S furry face doesn't give anything away, he simply walks back and forth like he doesn't have a care in the world. "I would love to take you up on that offer, Commander, but I have orders of my own. All you have to do is stand back and let us take SiN off your hands. I give you my word that we will bring back his pieces once we are finished with him."

· · ·

I'M SHOCKED when XuL is the first to pull his ax and step forward. "He is ours, and right or wrong he is not yours to take. Little female, I need you to come to me." He waves her towards him, and I make myself let her go. He is a mated male, and I know he will protect her with his life. Releasing her hand, I motion her to go to him. She looks up at me and I swear I can feel her confusion and the terror that is overcoming her mind. XuL's features are harsh and I'm sure that alone is scaring her. I nod for her to go to him and just as she takes a step, Qyinn speaks up.

"FEMALE, you will remain where you are. Three against the many is not a smart move for you no matter how skilled you and your sons are, Commander. Tell your sons to stand down, we bear you no ill will. SiN owes my superiors a significant number of credits, not including payment for the soldiers we lost regretfully on Targres Four. I will not be leaving this planet without him, that is unless you want to pay his debts."

JADE STEPS BACK TOWARDS ME, and that's when I know I'm going to have to take matters into my own hands. I don't understand the sudden pull I have towards her since I ingested her blood, but all I can think of is getting her out of here. Reaching down, I grab her wrist, then her ankle, picking her up like a rag doll. "Forgive me," I whisper as I swing her towards XuL. "Catch!" Her scream echoes throughout the clearing as her small body flies through the air.

PUSHING RaZ out of the way, I launch myself at the pirates before me. I become a shadow of vengeance. I don't know whose freedom I am fighting for, hers or mine, but I take advantage of the distraction my father and brothers create as I wreak death upon the ones who are here to capture me.

THE SHADOWS and my mist become one as I battle against the sheer numbers that keep appearing. Taking a hit to my already burned side, my mist dissipates for a moment and that's when I notice Father and RaZ are also battling a large number of pirates. XuL is nowhere in sight, and I hope that's because he has taken the female to safety.

THE FEELING of her terror in my mind instantly cuts off and I roar out. I have no idea what this means, but it's like the link that has pulled me towards her is suddenly severed. I throw bodies out of the way and start into the forest to find her, when it seems like time slows down, and I see it.

FATHER IS BEING overrun by the pack of Jynrel. His ax is swinging wildly as he cuts his way through the soldiers in front of him. He has a smile on his face even against such odds. His Symbots are twirling all over his body, protecting him from the many hands attacking him all at once. RaZ has his back to us, battling a few on his own. His large wings decapitate any that get too close, but the pirate's sheer numbers are overwhelming both males. For the first time I'm torn, do I pursue her or help them?

THE JYNREL ARE A WILD, vicious bunch who love to battle. Their bodies and natural enhancements make them deadly, especially if the pack works together as they are right now.

JUST AS I turn towards the forest and Jade. I catch movement out of the corner of my eye. A glimpse of something silver flashes in one of the trees above father. My mind sees the outcome before the pirate even has time to pull the trigger on the Lazer Phaser. Without a second thought, I appear between Father and the pirate who is trying to take a cheap shot at him. My body is thrown backwards from the compression hitting me in the chest. I look up when I hear a scream above me only to find a knife sticking through the eye of the pirate who just fired at me. Crumbling to the ground, the last thing I see before the darkness takes me is scared violet eyes, and the sound of my father's rage.

Chapter Eleven

SiN

Jᴇʀᴋɪɴɢ ᴀᴡᴀᴋᴇ ʟᴀᴛᴇʀ, I find myself lying on a hard bed in a dark gray room. Sitting up, I sway weakly as I swing my legs over the side. My movement must have triggered a sensor because the room starts to lighten. However, there is no missing the bars only a few feet in front of me.

Oɴ ᴜɴsᴛᴇᴀᴅʏ ʟᴇɢs, I approach them, and just as I start to reach out, a voice comes out of the darkness. "I wouldn't do that if I were you." RaZ strolls up with several red bags in his hand.

. . .

"You know these bars will not hold me. Why would you waste your time putting me in a location like this? What happened to the Jynrel and the female?"

"Demanding comes easy to you, doesn't it? Too bad you're in no shape to act on it." He points at the bars in front of me. "I think you will be surprised at what these little beauties will hold, SiN. Go ahead, grab one, I will happily stand back and watch the show." When I hesitate, he laughs. "That's the smartest thing I have seen you do yet. After the last stunt you pulled where you almost killed half the planet, we had this little spot prepared just for you. Danny reinforced the bars and the walls himself. It was obvious you didn't particularly care for his hold on you the last time."

"You can't keep me here forever," I snarl out.

"We can do whatever we want, but it's not been decided on exactly what your sentence will be yet. Unfortunately, because of that, technically, we have to keep you alive. So here. Newbies need to feed quite a bit in the beginning. Welcome to the fang club."

. . .

He slings the two bags at me, and they hit me right in the chest as I don't even try to catch them. Glancing down, they appear to be holding a red fluid.

"What is this madness?" I point down.

"Your dinner. It will taste like dirt, but it will keep you from settling into a death sleep."

"What are you talking about?"

RaZ points at my face. "Just got those didn't ya? You're a new fanger and you have no idea what that means. They will only retreat back into your gums when well-fed. If your mate is close, or you're hungry, they will emerge at will, as you will crave her like no other. Personally, I like mine, so they tend to stay put." RaZ clicks his tongue against his large fang and then smiles.

Leaving the bags on the ground, I turn back towards the bed. "It's nice to know you have my best interest at heart, dear brother, but you are wasting your time. I crave nothing, nor anyone, besides father's slow demise at my own hand."

.   .   .

"IF THAT'S THE CASE, why did you step in front of Father when that coward took that cheap shot at him from the tree? Let me think, what does my mate say … Oh yeah, I'm calling bullshit on that *I care for no one* act of yours. You just keep telling yourself that taking Father out is the only thing on your mind now that you have held your fated mate in your arms. It makes no difference to me one way or another what you want or if you even survive the next rising. I wouldn't be down here in the first place if it wasn't for Father." He starts laughing when I snarl at him. "This news is really going to burst your bubble SiN, because you owe Father's quick thinking to the fact that you are still with us."

"THINK WHAT YOU WANT, RaZ, my motives are mine alone. I am going to assume you defeated the Jynrel or we would not be having this conversation. With that being said, where is the female that was with me, did XuL get her to safety?"

"OH, YOU MEAN YOUR MATE?"

"DON'T BE RIDICULOUS. I have no mate."

.   .   .

"REALLY, because those fangs you have never sported before, tell me another story. I bet it's just eating you alive, knowing you're mentally and physically dependent on another right now. First lesson, your mind is no longer yours alone since you bit her. Thankfully, your female is not the same species as us and she cannot feel you the way you do her. I can't imagine any poor soul being tied to you for eternity. That would be an unbearable torture for even the strongest of souls. At least the bond is only one-sided right now. So, she will be no wiser to your demise, but you will know and feel everything she does once the bond fully forms."

RUBBING MY CHEST ABSENTMINDEDLY, my mind seeks her out involuntarily. Only the link seems muffled like it's a long distance away. "Where is she?"

RAZ LOOKS AWAY from me and I'm immediately back on my feet, grabbing the bars before I think about it. The electrical force hits me so hard my entire body mist apart in agony before reforming. Panting, I scream out. "Tell me! What have you done with her?"

HE TURNS his back to me and walks out of the room, his large wings scraping the floor as he goes. I roar out in anger at the sudden helplessness I feel being trapped in this cell. Fear hits me and I crumble to my knees only to realize it's not my fear I'm feeling, it's hers.

"FATHER!" I scream his name until my voice goes hoarse. Grabbing the bars over and over until the pain takes over my mind and I collapse to the floor. That's where he finds me when he finally decides to show up.

THE BARS DISAPPEAR and he walks in, but I'm too weak to get up. He grabs me under my arms and practically throws me onto the cot. My back hits the wall and I lean sideways upon it, too weak to move. My hatred for him rages through my mind as he stands before me.

WHEN HE LOOKS down at my chest, his eyes flash a bright red as his runes dance all over his skin. It appears that dear old dad is agitated. I can't help but laugh as he stands above me, larger than life.

"WHY DIDN'T you allow me to die if you were simply going to let me waste away in this room, or prison cell?"

· · ·

"Why did you step between me and that laser phaser? I thought that destroying me was your lifelong goal?"

"How long have I been here? Where is the female?"

"I won't answer a single thing until you do and we're running out of time if you want to save her, so get to talking."

"You won't obtain anything you desire from me."

"It's unfortunate to hear that, SiN. Is that your final answer?"

I look away; I owe him nothing. He grabs me by the shoulders, pushing me back against the wall. His fangs lengthen the same as mine as he growls down at me. Pulling the shadows around me, I draw what strength I have left and force him back until I'm back on my feet standing nose to nose with him.

His Symbots start walking up my arms, pulsing from him to me. He shoves me away, and I hit the wall again. His

Symbots retreat back to his arms, all but a small piece that seems to have wrapped themselves around my wrist. I tug on them, but they won't release. Just as I start to say something, he holds his hand up stopping me.

"YOU MIGHT AS WELL QUIT FIGHTING them, once they choose you, they're yours until your death. You should be grateful, they're the reason you survived the shot you willingly took for me. There was a hole in your chest as big as my fist. I called out for SCOUT to send a med bot the moment I realized you were so gravely injured, but I knew there was no way it would make it in time. The second I grabbed you to put pressure on your wound, I don't know who was more shocked, me or RaZ, when my Symbots left my body and merged into yours.

"SCOUT BELIEVES this occurred because our genetics are so close, and they couldn't tell the difference between us because of our proximity. They sealed the wound long enough for the med bot to finish the job when it arrived. The moment you were stable, the bulk of them returned to me, but as you can see, several decided to stay with you. My Kira was also chosen by them and is similarly marked."

"WHY WOULD you let them heal me? If I had died out there, it would have saved you the trouble of killing me later."

. . .

"Good question. All I can say is that I simply reacted, a trait I believe we have in common. You have much to answer for, SiN. The attack on Solanar is the first of many atrocities you have done to me and this family."

"Yeah, yeah, and Father, before you get all high and mighty on me, in my defense, I didn't know SCOUT could take on a physical form and I sure as frack didn't know that huge ass soldier was him in the flesh. I only set that EMP bomb to keep any of the other shuttles from leaving the area if things got out of hand, and they did quickly thanks to ViN and XuL crashing my party. And let's not forget to mention that girl said nothing about being mated to one of my brothers."

"She thought you were me, you idiot."

"Yes, I know, and that has worked to my advantage up until here lately. None of my spies reported that ViN was able to throw lava balls, and let me tell you, little brother has one hell of an aim. I'm still not sure how I recovered from that."

. . .

"I CAN TELL YOU HOW. According to Mystic, the human female is who healed you. Apparently, she figured out that her blood would do that by accident when her hand got cut just as Solanar crushed roughly onto Mystic. You were all seconds from being crushed by Solanar, which was solely your fault, by the way. When she covered your unconscious body with her own, trying to protect you. Something I don't believe you would have done for her if the tables had been turned. As she was trying to keep a hold of you, her hand came in contact with your bare skin.

"YOUR BODY ABSORBED her blood's nutrients directly through your skin. Right now, the only answer we can come up with is that this part of my genetics had simply laid dormant in your system until then. That's why your fangs appeared, and her blood healed you. When you ingest her blood straight into your system, you tied her to you for life. There is no escaping a blood bond. Time can lessen its pull, but even then, if you focus upon it, you can feel it … or them."

"SOUNDS like you have firsthand experience with this. Did you chew on a few necks when you were younger and now regret it, Father?"

. . .

"Regret is not the word I would choose. I did love another at one time and I craved her differently than I do My Kira now. Many times, the bond was just a constant reminder of what I had lost."

"I have no interest in your previous love life, Father, or anything else about you, for that matter. We are nothing alike, no matter what your fancy machines tell you. Don't waste your time trying to figure out my actions, now or in the future. And you are delusional if you think at any point I did any of it for you. I always have my reasons, but I am curious as to how long you've known I was staying with Mystic?"

"Shortly after you arrived rotations ago. At the time, of course, I didn't know who you were. Mystic kept your identity a secret this entire time."

"So you are saying even once you learned of my existence and all the things I was doing or had done, you never once tried to capture me knowing I was there."

He actually laughs. "You ever tried to fight a tree? Because I will inform you, unless she wanted you to be taken, no one, or thing, would have been able to pull you out of her arms. I knew at some point you would screw up, then we would cross paths, and here we are. However, it took almost losing your own life, destroying Mystic and let's not forget the sacrifice your sister made for you to finally come to your senses."

"SO, YOU KNOW ABOUT ELLARIA?"

"I HAVE LIMITED knowledge about what happened. I know that you were unconscious and what part the female played in all of it. Hopefully, she will be able to fill in the missing pieces about Ellaria when we locate her."

"YOU STILL HAVE NOT TOLD me where she is."

"IT'S because we don't know."

I HAVE him around the throat, holding him above the ground before he finishes his next sentence. He doesn't even fight me, just hangs there like dead weight. His eyes flashing red is the only sign of his emotions. "I am going to ask this once more and this time I want a different answer."

· · ·

LOWERING him back down to where his feet are touching the ground, I step back, releasing him, ready for a fight.

"WE DON'T KNOW."

BEFORE I CAN ATTACK him again something wraps around me, my body convulsing as my mist is torn apart and placed back together. "Danny, let him go," I hear Father say right before I hit the floor.

PUSHING myself up on shaky arms, I glance over at the young male standing just outside the cell. "Frack, I'm sick of you, little human. One of these days, I'm going to tear you apart."

"ANYTIME YOU'RE ready to get your ass kicked, SiN, you bring it on, mist boy. You haven't got the best of me yet, but you're more than welcome to give it another shot whenever you're up to it."

I ALMOST SMILE AT HIM, his attitude reminds me of myself at his age. Father stands in-between us like that youngling needs his protection.

. . .

"Danny, what are you doing here? I asked Tordan to take over your lessons this rising."

"And he did, Commander, but I asked to leave early. I have been here the whole time, even with RaZ earlier. I was concerned SiN might attempt to escape and harm one of the girls. Also, Katherine wants to speak with him, and I told her I would ask you."

Getting back to my feet, I stumble back to the cot and flop back down. My body has been pushed to its limits these last risings and I'm starving. "If you are planning on keeping me here, will you at least feed me?"

The bags of red fluid land on my chest. "For the next few risings, this is all your body will be able to hold down. I will have RaZ bring you more later, as your system will burn it up quickly."

Laying down, I push them to the side and sling my arm over my face as I'm done with these heart-to-heart conversations. "If you are not going to tell me what happened to the female, then leave. I have nothing left to say to you."

. . .

"I was hoping you would be able to tell me."

"How would I know? The last time I saw her I was literally tossing her to XuL."

"He got jumped by several of the Jynrels as he caught her, and she ran the moment her feet hit the ground. Originally, we hoped she had found her way back to one of the guardians, but that wasn't the case. SCOUT's scanners picked up her unconscious form being loaded onto the Jynrel ship shortly after they attacked us. It seems that Qyinn also escaped, as we didn't find his body with the others."

"I was heading into the forest when I saw that male in the trees above you. I felt her one moment and then the next she was gone. Since waking up in these amazing accommodations you've provided, I've been experiencing random emotions."

"Can you feel her now?"

"I'm not sure what that means."

.   .   .

"Do you feel drawn to a certain location? None of us know where the Jynrel sell the majority of their spoils. I never put a lot of time into their activities because they normally stay out of my territories. Their main operation is in ZoD's sector, and I have left them for him to deal with. If you can give us a direction, I will postpone your hearing with the elders in order for us to find her. If you feel nothing, then you need to prepare yourself for trial."

"How do I pinpoint something as odd as a feeling? And why do you care so much? She is just a random female."

"All females are sacred. I promised my mate I would protect her kind, and I keep my word. You act as if she is not important to you, but I know better. A mate bond will tear you apart from the inside, especially in your case where the bond has not been fulfilled."

"You talk nonsense. The female was sent to spy on me, if not from you, then from another. She holds no value other than the blood pumping through her system that I intend to drain entirely after I find out what I can from her."

.   .   .

"You are a fool, SiN. I saw it even if you couldn't, just from the way you were holding her in your arms. Son don't throw away the gifts the Lord of Light bestows upon you. Your hatred is unwarranted, and she has done nothing to deserve your wrath."

"All this talk of mates. You are all idiots to become so beholden to another. You, of all people, should know first-hand how easily the female mind can be turned. I will sever this tie and regain my freedom one way or another. If the female survives and is as innocent as you believe, then she will be glad to be rid of me."

He runs a hand through his hair, agitated by my constant disregard of the situation.

"All I need is a direction, SiN. It's a big universe out there and right now we are flying blindly, heading on no particular course. If you can provide me with something, we will leave within the hour."

We both turn our heads towards the opening of the cell when a female suddenly appears.

.   .   .

"Give me a moment with him, DaR. He doesn't know what to look for, as this is all new to him. He doesn't realize he can see the link that has tied them together. There are many things he needs to open his eyes to if he wants to save her and himself. Sometimes the truth has to be witnessed, not told."

Father nods his head. "I will be right outside, yell if you need me."

I sit up in the bed and wave her over. "Well, hello there, come right on in you pretty little thing, where have you been hiding? Frack if I don't feel important this rising. Look at all the company I am getting. I don't believe I have ever spoken to this many individuals in one rising. Why don't you come on over here and sit on my lap, I think I may need a personal demonstration."

Chapter Twelve

SiN

I KNOW the moment the female walks into the room who she belongs to. I can smell him on her, but I will play this game as long as I can. No cell has ever held me, and in time, this one won't either.

"I'M NOT sure what circumstances brought you to me, but frack, little human, you are a beauty."

"THANK YOU FOR THE COMPLIMENT, SiN, but enough of your flirting. I'm not here on a social call, there are things you need to know, and we don't have much time. All your actions up to this moment in time have been because you were falsely informed and because I told your sister I would. I am here to show you the truth."

"My sister is gone from this world."

"How do you know this?"

"Mystic showed me."

"And you believed the images she showed you?"

"Yes."

"Then this will not shock you."

Suddenly, I can't move. The female approaches me, her body hovering above the ground, her eyes glowing an eerie white. I struggle, but an unknown force is holding me in place. She touches a single finger to my forehead, and the images start. I find myself in a place I have never seen before. A small hand holding my own gently pulling me forward. When I glance down at who is holding my hand so familiarly, shocked to see it is Ellaria.

"Come, brother, you need to witness the falsehoods that have haunted your existence. I show you these things in the hope that you will find another path, and the chance to redeem yourself."

It's like I'm watching or living in a very realistic Holo screen. I can smell the scents in the air and feel the warmth of the sun's rays coming through the edges of the pulled curtains. A door suddenly opens and in walks DaR. I start to pull away from the hand not wanting to watch anything that he is involved in, but once again I can't move.

A female comes out of another door, running into his arms. I recognize her immediately, it's my aunt. The one person who was always good to me until I turned from her, as well. The scene seems too fast forward and things start to get all jumbled up. A curtain moves and my mother peers around it as she watches them together. Hatred, plain on her face, but it doesn't seem to be projected towards DaR like I expected.

She looks at him dreamily, her anger being directed towards her sister, my aunt Serena.

Serena leaves the room and DaR strips his clothes off, apparently planning on getting lucky. "I really don't want to see this, Ellaria."

"Watch."

A side door opens, and I expect my aunt to walk back in, but instead it's my mother. Somehow, she has glamoured herself and is now appearing before him as her sister. My first thought when I see the cloak around her natural form is, *He wasn't lying about this*.

The scene fast forwards again, and there is no missing the love DaR has for my aunt at this time. Soft words and gentle hands show how much he cares as he takes her maidenhead for his own. He speaks softly to her about the lives they are going to build together and his love. That is, until the real Serena walks back in the door. A cry leaves her quivering lips when she sees them together in front of her. Her face portrays all of her emotions, from betrayal, to disgust, to heartbreak. She turns, running from the room, crying.

. . .

DaR seems confused, he looks at the woman impaled upon his cock and then towards the one crying in the doorway. My mother Semora laughs like the madwoman she is, as their combined fluids run down her thighs. I can't hear her words, but I can tell his reaction is not what she expected.

DaR throws her off him, scrambling to get dressed, as he races after my aunt Serena, screaming out her name. However, the sad story doesn't end there. The second DaR leaves the room, we follow my mother through a hidden panel in the wall. Walking quickly, she holds her hand against her feminine opening, making sure nothing is escaping her channel.

There is an unknown male waiting for her, but I can't see his face clearly. He helps her up onto a table gently. They are unusually comfortable with each other, so I can tell this is not the first time they have been intimate. He pulls DaR's fluids out of her carefully, placing small amounts of it into cups before inserting them in a machine.

"Semora, your sister's eggs are ready and if his sperm is still active. We should be able to inseminate these into you successfully. Your uterus is healthy enough to carry the embryos to full term, even with your ovaries being defective. The similarities between you and your sister are so similar that no one will ever know you carry her child instead of your own. Unless you tell them, or the child is tested.

"THIS PLAN of yours was quite ingenious, Semora. I can't believe he couldn't see through your disguise. You were wise to use his lust against him. I will say I am impressed with how effortlessly you pulled all of this off. There were so many things that could go wrong, and you have succeeded where many would have failed. The fact that you were able to drug your sister last rising and successfully remove all the eggs she will ever produce is impressive. Then getting his essence before her eggs expired shows how determined you were.

"IF THIS PROCEDURE IS SUCCESSFUL, I will freeze the remainder of his sperm for you to sell at a later date. If DaR becomes a commander, his sperm will be worth top credits, and that should provide quite a bit of wealth for you and the child."

I WATCH as mother snarls at him, distorting her beauty showing her true face. "I could care less about the credits. My family will make sure I am always provided for.

However, the moment DaR is informed I carry his child, he will bind himself to me and I will finally have the male I have coveted for rotations. DaR may not care for me in the beginning, but I have my ways, as you can tell. Do with the extra however you want once we know this procedure is successful. How long will it take before we know if this was a success?"

"IT SHOULD BE NO MORE than two rotations. From that point on, normal procedures can be provided for you without me overseeing them. You will be able to proceed like you got pregnant naturally, with no one the wiser."

SAMORA LAUGHS, her eyes showing the madness she tries to hide from the world. "I know the moment he finds out I am pregnant with his child, he will accept me. His honor demands it. Then we will see how my sister enjoys watching another's happiness from the sidelines. DaR should have been mine from the beginning, but my sister blinded him with her fake grace and innocence. I will provide him with pleasures and power he never dreamed of one way or another."

THE SCENE CHANGES AGAIN, but this time I recognize the fury on my mother's face, as this is all I was ever shown. She is heavily pregnant, throwing things and ranting as she tries to leave a room she seems to be trapped in. A door opens suddenly and in walks Serena.

"Sister, calm yourself before you damage the children."

"What do you care, you have poisoned our parental units against me. Blocked all the communication stations so that I can't contact DaR and tell him about his children. It's all your fault I'm being sent away. They have always cared for you more than me."

"Semora, that's not true, and you being sent away is your own fault. You know Father would never allow a scandal such as this to slander the family name. I have no idea what you thought that little stunt of yours would prove, but all you have done is ruin all three of our lives. You are not the only one being forced to do something she doesn't want to do. At least he isn't forcing you to marry another to simply remove you from the dwelling. Once the children are born you can still pick another if you wish. Your actions took that choice from me."

"Ohhh, please Serena, you poor little thing. DaR would have run into your arms and taken you back in a heartbeat."

. . .

"Possibly, but I can never unsee what I did. The thought of him touching me after you disgusts me and even my continued love for him cannot fix that. So, with a heavy heart, I set him free to pursue the career he was always meant to have."

"If DaR knew I was carrying his children, he wouldn't allow you to treat me like this. He would take me away from here and you."

"Semora, how do we know if it's his child? You have spread your legs for so many already. I saw the blood on your clothing where you cut yourself so DaR would believe he took your innocence but quit lying because we both know better. You will raise these children elsewhere and never return. It doesn't matter who the father is, this is your mistake, and others should not be made to pay for your trickery. Now grow up and do the right thing.

"Sister, this will be the last time I will see you until after the children are born. I hope that you find some type of happiness in the life you have chosen for yourself and the little ones you carry."

. . .

THE NEXT SCENE shows Mother giving birth. There are med bots running all over the place as she screams out one last time. I watch as two younglings are cleaned and laid together in another area. Ellaria pulls me closer to a floating crib and points down.

THE TWO YOUNGLINGS are snuggled together. The larger one is holding onto the smaller one as it struggles to breathe. Mother walks over, tearing them apart holding the male up … me. She looks me over with a wicked grin on her face.

"OH LOOK AT YOU, already you are the spitting image of him. The plans I have for us, my son, will change history. You will be my greatest weapon and my revenge on them all."

THE MED BOT holds the smaller one up to Mother and she turns away, snarling. "Kill it, I won't be haunted by the face of my sister every rising."

WHEN THE MED BOT REFUSES, I watch in horror as she reaches over, tearing the wires out of it. The cries in the crib get weaker as the rising goes on until they are no more. My heart breaks when Ellaria squeezes my hand, still trying to comfort me all these risings later. If Ellaria had lived, I wonder what nightmare my mother would have made her into or if she'd just been another to abuse.

THEN ONE SCENE after another shows the things mother did to me. How she created the perfect reproduction of the man she loved and hated all the same. Her infatuation with DaR became a dark, angry obsession that turned into revenge the moment I appeared. She saw me as nothing but a tool to use against the ones she felt had wronged her.

THESE SCENES SHOW me going from a quiet child to a bitter male, and how all of this was just a way for her to get back at him through me. When she took her own life, I blamed that on him too. The few times I saw Ellaria was when we were both small. What I didn't realize, was always when my aunt was close by. I flinch as I watch how I treated her, or ignored her, until one rising she too was gone.

EVERYTHING I HAVE BEEN TAUGHT WAS false ... a lie. My aunt tried to tell me many times that things were not as they seemed. I refused to listen when she told me to ask my mother for the truth.

. . .

WHAT HAVE I DONE? Look at who all has suffered because of her madness. Madness that I took on as my own? Ellaria fades away and I find myself back in the cell. My heart is heavy as my actions weigh heavily upon me. The female that Ellaria has used to show me in the past now sits on the bed beside me, holding my hand gently.

"I'M SORRY SIN, even I didn't realize what happened or the circumstances that led you to be the way you are. I know the scenes Ellaria had me show you are tearing you up inside, but you cannot change the past, only the future. These next moments in time will decide your path. I hope that for once you can set aside the hatred you were fed and look inside for the male you want to be."

"DOES HE KNOW THE WHOLE TRUTH?"

"YOU MEAN DAR?"

"YES."

"No, and until now, I didn't either."

. . .

"WILL YOU TELL HIM?"

"THIS IS NOT my story to tell. If you ever want him to know the facts, the words will have to come from your lips, not mine. I will verify it if he questions you, though. Him knowing the truth will not change the past SiN, but it could cause issues in the future. Think about the consequences before you act. DaR and your aunt have both moved on with their lives. Revealing this just might do the one thing your mother wanted and destroy them both. Going back won't change the things that happened to you, it won't change the things that you have done or that others did to you. That's why it's called the past.

"IF YOU ARE STILL willing to try. I will show you how to grab onto the link that pulls you and Jade together. SiN, I wish there was a way to give you some time to sort through all this, but we don't have that luxury. You are Jade's only hope at this point."

"WILL I ever see my sister again, little female? I am ashamed of … well everything. She haunted me from the time we were little and until recently I had no idea who she even was. Even hearing the truth straight from Father's lips, I still refused to believe it. I owe Ellaria the few fleeting moments of my childhood happiness. So much pain, and so many lives changed all because of the insanity of one female. She never really hated him. I can see that now. She simply wanted what they had, love. In her madness, she couldn't see past her own wants."

My thoughts take me away for a moment, only her standing up and taking her comforting presence away from my side makes me come back to myself. I reach out, grabbing her hand gently. "Thank you for doing this for her, for me. What is your name?"

"It's Katherine, I will give you a moment to yourself, then I will be back. All I ask of you, SiN, is to remember what your sister gave up so that you have the chance she never had. Don't waste Ellaria's sacrifice. You both still have a chance for happiness. Look past what you are and strive to be something else … more. If not for yourself, then do it for your sister, your aunt, maybe Jade, or even your father. I know I have said this before, but you cannot change the past, only your future. Trust me, I understand how sad that statement is."

DaR … Father walks back into the room and this is when I notice they had not turned the bars back on. My first thought is. *I could leave right now, neither one of them have the power to stop me. All I need to do is find a way out of here.* Hide out, until I figure out what to do next, but isn't that what I have been doing for risings now? Just reacting, all my choices and bad decisions have led me here to this crossroads in my life.

My aunt once said, *It's easy to be bad, SiN. You have to work at being good.* She kissed me on the cheek, and I watched her walk away that rising. I have not sought her out nor seen her since. I wonder now if it pained her to look upon me, as mine and Father's features are almost identical.

How would she see me if she knew the truth? Would she try to be the mother I never had, or would I have been a constant reminder of what she could have had? I wonder if I would have been an honorable male if she had been the one to carry and raise me? Or was I always destined to be the opposite of the male standing in front of me now? So many questions, so many what ifs.

I look up at him for the first time and see the lines that contour his face. The weight of the world and the choices he has had to make to keep the ones he loved safe. Many times, he has allowed me to approach him. He has allowed me to slander his name. Even taking my crimes as his own, especially when I was impersonating him. I almost got his best friend killed, and he still hesitated, just as he does now. Is that a father's love?

IT's difficult to imagine the suffering he experienced when he lost Serena. I saw their love firsthand. I don't know if I could have accepted her decision if it had been me. When she married and left Darverius, he had to have felt like his heart was being ripped out.

THE LORD OF LIGHT knows how I have hated him and the others born after me. Now that I see the story clearer, I realize my anger was driven by jealousy. He gave his love freely to his other sons, but not me. He saved XuL and took SoL in with no questions asked. I always wondered why he didn't come for me. With each rotation, I hated him more for leaving me there … with her. My whole life has been a lie that I blamed on him.

CLOSING MY EYES, I squeeze the small hand still holding mine gently, my heart and mind heavy. "Katherine, there has been enough pain in my life already. I won't allow another to suffer because of my own failures. Tell me what to do."

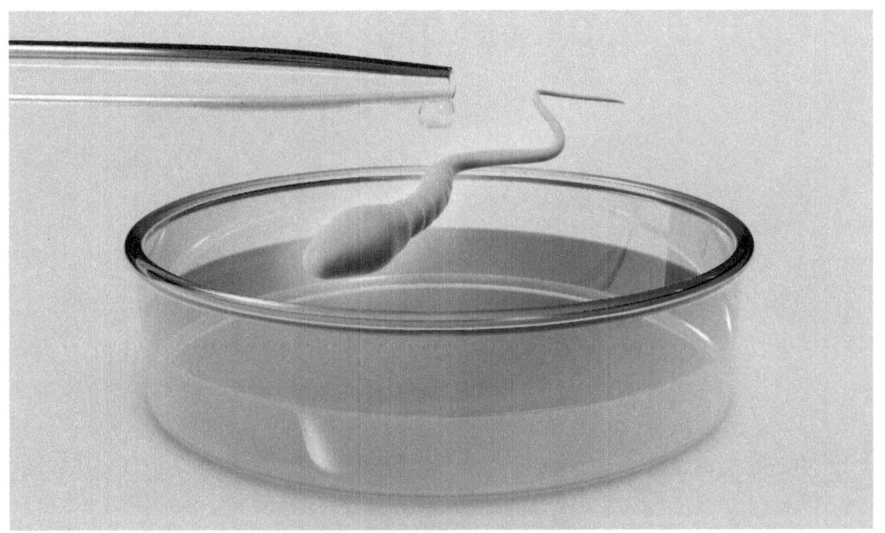

Chapter Thirteen

Jade

God, I'm tired of waking up in strange places, and once again. I have no idea where I am or how I got here. The last thing I remember is SiN unexpectedly throwing me towards the big green guy he had just spoken to. I think the guy caught me, but besides running the moment he sat me down, I don't recall anything else. Wiggling my fingers and toes, I appear to still have all my parts and I don't seem any worse off than I was before.

My nose curls up in disgust as this place smells like wet dogs and stinky feet. I try to move, but once again, I find myself strapped down onto a hard surface. Refusing to flip out, I lie here, looking around at the apparent medical room I'm being held in. Cringing every time I hear footsteps approaching. Why do I feel like this has happened to me before?

A DOORWAY OPENS in front of me and then closes back quickly, but not before I notice another alien standing there yelling at someone I can't see clearly.

THE ONE I catch a glimpse of, is massive to the point he looks unreal, or unlike anything I can even fathom. His snow-white skin is marked by an array of dark tattoos. His coloring stands out brightly in all the gloominess behind him. Even though they are talking loudly, I can't make out anything besides the word female.

HELPLESS, I start shaking, my body awakening enough to realize I'm in serious trouble, and this time I don't believe a nice tree is going to save me. The doorway reopens and my eyes widen at the creature that comes waddling in, mumbling the word *unacceptable* under its breath.

THE CREATURE CAN'T BE MUCH LARGER than I am in height, but that's where all our similarities end. It's pale brown with a head so large I have no idea how its neck is holding it up, and all those eyes are just downright creepy. Six of them seem to be going in all different directions at once, seeing everything, as it continues to talk to itself. I can't help but scream when one of its four arms reaches up, touching me.

WHEN IT TURNS all of those eyes in my direction, I wish I had kept my mouth shut. One creepy-ass hand holds down my head while another pokes and probes behind my ear. I push away as far as the restraints will let me, but can't help from screaming out in pain when it feels like it's ripping my ear off.

IT FINALLY LETS GO of me and before I can even catch my breath, another pale brown hand is covering my face. Gasping, I see what appears to be bubbles in the air above me, then nothing. What feels like seconds later I wake right back up. The same creep with the eyeballs is still standing over me.

"FEMALE, CAN YOU UNDERSTAND ME?"

I SHAKE MY HEAD YES, too scared to talk.

•   •   •

"You are free to speak to me as you wish. I actually would appreciate any and all conversation, as this will make my study of your species more accurate. As of this time, my superiors have placed me here to observe you." One of its many hands pats my arm gently.

His words don't match his lips, so some of the words break up or don't sound right together. "Can I ask what you are?"

"I am a certified research and care provider for this facility."

"No, I mean what are you?"

"Pardon me, I thought you were asking for my credentials. I am of the race Chilten. We are the holders of knowledge in this sector and often work on projects that others shy from. I am your personal handler, and no other will enter into this suite besides myself. There is a viewing platform above where we can be monitored, but at this time your species has not been deemed unique enough for possible breeders or buyers."

"I take it I'm not the first of my kind to be brought here?"

. . .

"Correct, I hope to have better success with you than the others had with their subjects. I am pleased that you seem to be handling your change of venue without the usual hysterics. This keeps me from having to use further restraints. I would like to apologize for the unnecessary pain I caused you earlier. I was attempting to reset your translator only to find out that the one you had inserted was faulty. The defective unit has been removed and a new model has been installed to facilitate our communication easier."

"So you don't plan on hurting me?"

"That is not my intent, but I know some of the things I am demanded to provide for my superiors, you will not be receptive of. However, I will do the courtesy of asking or telling you first, either way. I have already taken blood and some tissue samples while you were under. They are being processed as we speak. I was informed your blood may be poisonous to many species. So certain safety precautions have to be put in place until deemed one way or another. Once I get that test back, I will remove your restraints. As long as you don't become violent, you will be free to move around in here. Can I ask you a few questions while we wait?"

. . .

"Doesn't look like I'm going anywhere, but let me warn you, I can't recall anything past the last few days. As for my blood being poisonous, I have no idea where you would have heard that."

"Interesting that you would say that about your blood. It's one of the main reasons you are here. Recently we were able to intercept some research that was stolen from an AI on Targres Four about your species. My superiors are looking for a bioweapon, and there have been rumors that your kind might hold the key. We have also seen several cases where your blood has formed a mating bond. To be a primitive species, you have become a high commodity to the ones willing to take the chance at purchasing one of you. The sources of our information are credible, we simply have to prove the effectiveness of your blood before we can go any further. Until then, I have other inquiries about your species. Do you recall how these markings got upon your skin, or how you came to be on Darverius?"

"Nope. Every once in a while, I catch a fragment of a memory, but the moment I try to grab onto it, it's gone."

"Do you recall your name?"

. . .

"Yes, that I do remember. It's Becca Jade Simpson. You can call me Jade, everyone else does, I think."

"I am known as Volten, I am going to run a scan over you. You should feel nothing, but it may tell us why you have lost your memories."

He no more says that when a blue light runs from my head to my toes. His … I'm assuming it's a male; his multiple eyes seem to be reading different things all at once. It is like he is a super brain or something.

"Jade, the test is not complete yet, but from what I can tell already, you have been implanted with a memory blocker. Whoever installed it must have also been the one who gave you the translator because it too is faulty. I believe they were trying to erase their mark on you as quickly as possible, with no thought or care for your welfare.

"This may have happened when Commander DaR put out that he was personally protecting your species. Some were terrified of what would happen if a human was found in their residence. I fear many of your kind were destroyed unnecessarily by their instant haste to be rid of you. Especially when facilities such as this would have gladly taken them.

"I AM CONCERNED that if I remove it, you could go catatonic from the experiences that have marked your tender flesh. Your memories would race to the forefront of your cerebrum, overwhelming your pain sensors as you relived each event in seconds. The scars your body holds were not put there gently, but for my research to be accurate. I need you at full brain capacity. I will have to discuss this further with my other colleagues. At this time, we will leave things as they are.

"I DON'T KNOW this Commander DaR."

"HE IS OF NO CONCERN, as you are no longer in his sector and this facility is under another's command. His laws are not upheld in this sector. We previously purchased another female of your race, but the specimen was taken before we could retrieve it. Your fragile kind don't last long in our universe and this has made the owner of this facility extremely curious as to how your kind come to be here, and what your sudden appearance could mean. While we await the other test, I have several more questions. Then I will allow you to rest and provide substance for you at that time."

• • •

His questions go on and on. I answered what I could, but it's easy to tell he is aggravated with my answers. He becomes even more agitated when I ask about the dog-like things that brought me here, telling me that it was all my imagination, and my mind was messing with me. Right after that, he disappears abruptly, leaving me still strapped to the table.

I should take his word for it, my mind is a mess, but I remember them surrounding us in the clearing and SiN even acting like he was going to protect me for a moment. The thought of him makes my heart jump in my chest. I swear it's like I can feel him inside me, but I know that's just wishful thinking on my end. At this point, what girl wouldn't daydream that a male even one as aggressive as he was, would come to her rescue? Realistically, I know he won't look for me even if he did survive that attack. I am on my own, like I always have been.

The thought of him simply forgetting about me bothers me more than it should, though. It's probably because I watched over him while he was healing. In my head, I made up my own version of who and what he was. Only to once again be disappointed with reality when he awakened. His face remains vivid in my mind. I shake my head at my foolishness as I recall how his features would make a saint fall to their knees in worship. Such anger and distrust under all that beauty. All I got to witness firsthand was frowns and snarls. I can't picture what a transformation a smile would have done to his already perfect face. I probably would have melted to the ground in a pile of mush.

As I SQUIRM under the restraints, my mind is rushing with what has happened since I awakened here. Even though Volten is acting like he has my best interest at heart, I know it's a lie. Once again, I'm only a piece of flesh for someone or something to abuse. No one is coming to save me, so I need to play nice until I can save myself. I refuse to believe this was all I was ever meant for.

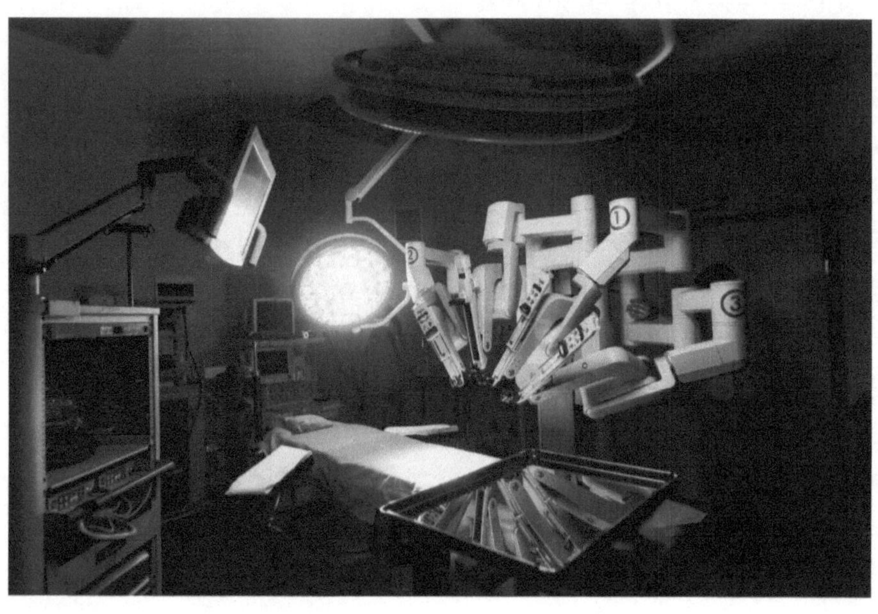

Chapter Fourteen

SiN

KATHERINE SIGHS ONCE AGAIN. "SiN, you are making this way harder than it is. Quiet your mind, and only think of her. You two have a blood link, and because she is the only one you have ever fed from, nothing should be blocking you from finding her. Picture a ribbon in your mind and try to connect it to the pull you're feeling."

SNARLING OUT, I can't think past the hunger consuming my thoughts. I clench my hands, trying to fight off these feelings, but everything is just too loud. Looking over at Katherine, the veins in her neck pulse to the point I can see the fluid running through them.

BEFORE I CAN GRAB her to satisfy this all-consuming hunger, I am seized from behind. I fight against the hold they have on me as they force me down onto the bed. Immediately, I try to mist away only to find I can't. This hunger has taken over my thoughts and my basic instincts.

RaZ ACTUALLY LAUGHS as Father practically sits on my stomach, forcing my lips open so they can dump that repulsive red liquid down my throat. Choking, I manage to swallow the first bag before they release me. Gagging from the taste, my mind starts to settle. Still laughing, RaZ throws the other bag on my lap.

"TOLD you it tasted like dirt; you should have listened to me. Now see if you can figure out this next one on your own."

I DON'T KNOW who is shocked more, me, or RaZ when Katherine suddenly sticks up for me. "Dammit, RaZ he has no idea what he is doing, lighten up."

. . .

"MY LOVE, save your sympathy for someone who deserves it. This dick is getting everything he deserves. If you hadn't shown up here, I would have let him suffer for a while longer. Nothing would have made me happier than to watch him convulse on the floor in agony before begging me to make it stop."

HE POINTS AT ME. "You can thank my mate for the kindness you have been shown during this transition. I gladly would have cut you down to size for the things you have done to Father and to Solanar if it was up to me."

"I HAVE a feeling you don't care much for me, brother."

HE SNARLS DOWN AT ME. His large wings quiver in anger on his back. "Don't call me that. You haven't earned that right. Family doesn't try to destroy each other, you frackin, idiot. Are you so blind you can't see who is here with you right now? Not your so-called buddies, or your hired thugs. Your frackin' family, DICK. You know, the ones you have tried to kill multiple times. So unless you want to take this to the next stage quickly … you call me brother again. Katherine, my love, wrap it up in here. I have stomached all of him I can for one rising."

. . .

FATHER HASN'T SAID A WORD. He just stands against the wall with his arms crossed, watching. RaZ stops in front of him for a second, they don't say a word, but I know they are talking to each other. It takes every ounce of my strength not to strike out like I always have. I know my hatred for all of them is unwarranted. I have seen the proof with my own eyes, but how do I just shut off all these emotions?

MY GUMS ache as I grit my new teeth together. As I struggle to fight the internal frenzy, my body is trying to force me into, Katherine sits back down beside me, shaking her head when I still can't seem to get the package open.

"I SWEAR, you all need to go somewhere and chill out. If the testosterone level gets any higher, or the air any thicker in here, we are all gonna suffocate. Go on RaZ, walk it off, I'll be fine."

HE TURNS back like he is going to argue with her. She just raises her eyebrows, giving him a look, then points to the door. A snarl leaves his lips and before I can blink, he is standing before her holding her hand. "What is this?"

.   .   .

"Not right now, RaZ … Don't give me that look. I promise I will tell you, just not right now."

"You know, I like it when you get all sassy on me. It seems like you're in need of a spanking, young lady. You know I don't like secrets."

"Looking forward to it, that is, if you can catch me."

Their easy banter back and forth makes me uncomfortable. Is this normal? Up to now, all a female was meant for in my eyes, was a quick release, and a wave goodbye as I was leaving. I am swimming in unknown territory here and I don't care much for it. After RaZ walks away, she turns all her attention back to me.

"Here SiN, take the bag like this and try to just use your fangs. You won't taste the blood that way, let your fangs do the work. It will take practice, but you will be a pro in no time."

I think this is the most humiliating thing that has ever happened to me. Several times I try to puncture the bag. When I finally do, I end up with the blood all over me again.

. . .

"GIVE IT HERE. Let me show you."

"WHAT, YOU, HOW?"

JUST AS GRACEFUL as can be, she gently pierces the bag, inserting a single fang.

"WAIT A MINUTE, YOU HAVE FANGS?"

"SURE DO, BIG GUY."

I WATCH in complete amazement when she smiles, and they retreat back up into her gums. I thought I knew everything about this family, but it seems I am mistaken. *How did my informants miss this?*

"WHAT THE FRACK? How? Where did they go? Did that damn winged bastard give those to you? Can we pass this curse on to others easily?"

. . .

"INTERESTED, I see. I'll answer all your questions as soon as you eat, SiN."

I PUNCTURE ANOTHER BAG, draining it quickly, only managing to get a little bit of it on my hands this time.

"YOU STILL FEEL shaky on the inside?"

"YEAH, it's weird. I am hungry, but the thought of food is disgusting."

"IT's because you fed from a human, it triggered a trait that was supposed to have been erased from your kind. You see, your race evolved differently than ours did on Earth. Until your grandfather and the others crashed on Earth, there were no such things as vampires or anything that fed on the blood of others currently there.

"IF THIS DORMANT trait of yours had awakened when you were a child, DaR would have given you a Blood Beat like his father did him when his appeared. The nectar in that fruit has a way of settling the craving, and solid food would still be your preferred sustenance. I am not sure at your age how your body will adjust. This may be the first of many traits that have laid dormant in your system until now. You may never be able to digest solid foods again. RaZ still has very little tolerance for solids himself and he has been dealing with this since birth.

"SINCE YOUR FIRST feeding was live and human, your situation is similar to RaZ's, in the sense that he bit his mother right after his birth. I hate to tell you this, but now Jade's blood is the only thing that will truly ever take away your hunger. You can survive on this synthetic blood, but the taste will always be terrible. Everyone has their own unique flavor, if you understand my meaning. Even if you bite another human, the taste may be slightly better than this, but nothing like your first.

"TYBERIUS AND VICTORIA had used synthetic blood for years when they were in public and trying to fit in. Yet, they still prefer the taste of each other over anything else. I personally still enjoy it straight from the tap, as I like to joke about it. RaZ is my true mate, the thought of having to feed from any other is just yucky. However, because of our mate status, our bodies produce enough to feed each other and let me tell ya, the fun that can lead to. I still enjoy solid food. I just don't require it."

. . .

"HOW LONG HAVE you been like this?"

"I WAS BORN A VAMPIRE, and so was Victoria. Pureblood births are rare, but that is also why I can pass as a normal human. I have ways of glamouring myself so that others only see what I want them to. Humans can be changed, but it's not always successful. The change is so drastic they have an extremely hard time blending in and often have to be put down because they couldn't control their thirst. As to where my fangs went. We had to learn to blend in on earth, evolve, if you will. We taught ourselves to hide in plain sight."

"I THOUGHT RaZ was a fool for leaving you here with me. I could have easily overpowered you and then used you to escape this place."

"OH, you could have tried, SiN. You should know better than most, looks can be deceiving. Most who gaze upon me only see a small-boned, fragile female, and I prefer it that way. Don't you worry, I have many tricks up my sleeve. I would have allowed you to believe you had me, until you didn't. Now, enough about me, I will go get you a few more bags of all that yuckiness in a little bit. Hopefully, it will help level out these emotions you are having, but we need to talk about Jade. You are responding to the start of a blood addiction. I'm hoping that craving alone will help you locate Jade. Her unique scent and taste should always call to you, no matter where or how far away she is."

"My feelings are all over the place, how do I sort through them to find her? I'm not used to being out of control like this. I know nothing about this Jade at all, it's like I'm looking for a stranger with blindfolds on."

"I didn't think about it like that. Still, I believe the reason you are so out of sorts is because her feelings are over-whelming your own. You need to find a way to separate the two. Do you have a happy place? Somewhere in your mind that you can escape to when the world becomes too much."

"Not really, I enjoy the chaos, thrive on it really."

Katherine shakes her head. "Of course you would. Ok then, we need to look at this another way then. How about scared, maybe a pain someplace that you are not used to, or possibly some type of confusion that you don't understand."

. . .

"Confusion, yes that's what is nagging at me. It's like I'm seeing something different than what is right in front of me."

"Grab onto that thought, now trace it with your mind. See where it's going. Do you have an urge to walk towards it? Stand up and close your eyes. Don't think about it, just walk."

As foolish as this seems. I do as she says, and it's like my mind drifts away from my body. For a split second, I can see through Jade's eyes. I feel her helplessness, and the fact that she is restrained. Something is speaking to her, but she is looking away, staring up at mechanical arms suspended above her. She squirms, trying to push away from them as they get lower. Panic absorbs her mind as multiple needles puncture her delicate skin and I feel them like it's happening to my body. Her thoughts become foggy, I don't know what is happening, but I can already feel her weakening.

I yank myself out of her mind's hold only to find that I have walked right up to Father. He still hasn't moved from the spot he has been leaning against, watching me and Katherine. He looks at me like he is searching for something. Eye to eye he stands before me, and I wonder if I should tell him the truth. Would he look at me differently, would he fight by my side to help save me from the sins I have committed against him and the others of my family? Ashamed and confused, I am the first to lower my gaze.

"KATHERINE, leave us. My son and I have much to discuss."

SHE GETS up off the cot where she had been talking to me and nods her head yes. Giving me a sad smile, she walks away. I turn back towards my cell, no longer having the urge to flee. Running is all I have done my entire life, but now I don't know how to go forward.

FATHER'S VOICE pulls me out of my own thoughts. "Come, let's take a walk."

Chapter Fifteen

SiN

I AM SHOCKED to see where they have been retaining me as we move through a doorway. I never dreamed Father would have taken the chance of holding me this close to his mate. He doesn't say a word as we walk along the perimeter wall, his own dwelling only feet away. Father steps up on the cliff that overlooks his original home where he raised the chosen ones. Sitting down, he motions for me to do the same.

HESITANTLY, I sit, looking out over the vast valley with Solanar floating peacefully over from us. The strength of Darverius sun's bearing down on me makes my skin itch and I have to fight the urge to simply mist away into the coolness of the Dark Forest. He doesn't say anything, just sits here looking around, with one knee up, his large arm resting carelessly on it like he doesn't have a care in the world.

"You are taking a tremendous risk in letting me out here, Father." With my hand, I motion around us. "In the open like this, there is nothing you could do to keep me here. I could mist away before you could blink an eye."

"True, but I was hoping for once you would restrain yourself. If not for your sake at least the female. Go ahead and leave if you must, SiN. We will simply come to this place again in the future and when that rising comes. My leniency with you will no longer exist."

I can't stop the growl that leaves my throat.

"For once, SiN, you need to put another's needs before yourself. Swallow your pride and help us find this female. Your world has changed. I can see it in your face and in the way you hesitate, not knowing how to proceed. None of us accept change well, you are no exception. If you could go back two risings ago and someone told you that you would be sitting here right now, with the male, you have always considered your biggest enemy. You would have fought the bearer of that news to the death. No amount of fighting or wishing changes the past or the future, son. I have done both many times and still time marches forward, even when you wish it didn't."

THE WAY he says the word son still rubs me wrong. I fight back the words that want to spill from my mouth as my mind wonders. As much as I hate to admit it, my world has changed. Before I knew my purpose in life, but now I'm suddenly floating around in the unknown. My risings are numbered, and I know even if I managed to elude Father right now, he is right. The moment I am caught again they will simply kill me on the spot or send that frackin human male to tear me apart from the inside out.

MYSTIC FOUND the little female worthy, and if I don't save the girl for any other reason, I should do it for her. She sheltered me when I had nothing or no one. This poor female simply got trapped in a war she was never meant to be in. The thought of facing the elders and answering for my wrongs bothers me more than it should. I never had dreams of the next rising, but I did take for granted that I was smarter than they all were. Possibly for a moment, I was, but either way here I am. His voice snaps me back to the present.

. . .

"This female will become a ghost in your heart SiN, if you don't finish or break the bond you have started with her. You will crave her and her love until you become obsessive and uncontrollable. It will be the complete death of your peace of mind. You cannot change the past only the future, son. This female does not deserve to suffer for your misdeeds. Those are yours alone to atone for, and you will answer for all that you have done. All this has done is prolong the inevitable. Will you be male enough to do the right thing this time, or is regressing into who you have always been more fulfilling?"

I snarl over at him, "You think you are so wise, so knowing. A male who lost so little and gained so much. How dare you stand here acting like I'm the only one to blame. You talk of the past like you had no part of it. How naïve of you, Father, because whether you want to admit it or not, I am your one and only sin. The son you walked away from; you are just as much to blame as I am. We waste time sitting here acting like all is well between us. I will help find the female, but don't think for one moment I do this for you."

Getting to my feet I almost bump into Tordan who I had no idea had been with us this entire time. "Standing in the shadow of my Father, still I see, oh mighty Tordan. I often wonder who I despise more, him or you. For something tells me you know more than you let on. If I am ever able to confirm that knowledge you better watch your back."

HE SAYS NOTHING, just smirks at me like he is laughing at my own ignorance. He leans around me to look at Father. "Commander, the Explorer is ready, all we await is you."

FATHER RUNS a hand through his long hair and a weary sigh leaves his lips. For a moment, he looks older and worn down until he gets to his feet. The male standing before me has built himself and the world I stand upon. His broad shoulders are all that keeps the ones who dwell here safe, and he knows this. He could push me off onto one of the others, but I know he won't and it's not because of what I done. It's who I am, his son, and right now I feel like a rebellious youngling.

FATHER TOUCHES the comm unit on his wrist. "SAGE, have Kira meet me at my shuttle, we will be departing momentarily."

A SOFT VOICE REPLIES. "YES, COMMANDER."

. . .

Tordan nods his head as he turns away from us. "DaR, I will meet you two on board."

Father shakes his head yes, then motions me towards his dwelling. "Wouldn't you prefer me to go with him?"

He stops suddenly, turning towards me. "SiN, I have taken personal responsibility for you with the elders. Even though I trust Tordan with my life. I won't place that burden on him in case you decide to be who you have always been. I can see the struggle in your eyes the moment someone new approaches you. No one is going to take it easy on you; respect and trust has to be earned. The question is? Are you male enough to handle this task, or would you rather wait in a cell? Tell me now because every person on that ship is putting their lives on the line to save this female and none are doing it for you."

He doesn't even give me a chance to respond before he turns away from me, and then I see the cause. His little mate, the female I have scared and tried to take from him several times has stepped out into the yard.

As he walks up to her, she gazes up at him so lovingly. Those old feelings come back with a vengeance and I glance towards the forest, my fingers misting on their own as my body prepares to flee. I glance back at them shocked to see her moving towards me. I start to step backward, but I know he is testing me to see what I will do. Even though I'm having to bite the inside of my jaw, I make myself stand still.

I GLARE at him and then back to the little female who is now only a few feet from me. My fangs start to ache the moment I smell her, but I force myself to think of something else.

SHE DOESN'T SAY ANYTHING, at first, she just stands here looking up at me. Inside my mind, I suddenly feel like she is tearing me apart, piece by piece. My wrist starts to itch and I reach down, trying to push the ring of Father Symbots off.

A SMALL HAND on my wrist stops me, I lean back away from her when she reaches up to touch my cheek. "You look so like him." She whispers and before I can reply, "It just dawned on me that we have never been properly introduced, I'm Kira. DaR told me there was no need for me to do this, but I felt like I needed to. I wanted to personally thank you for saving his life the other day. Your sacrifice just proved what I knew all along, but that is something me and you will talk about at a later date."

. . .

Before I could say another word, she wraps her arms around my waist, hugging me tightly. I hold my arms out straight and lean away from her immediately, looking at Father, expecting him to be preparing to tear my head off. Instead, he just stands there watching us both. Hesitantly, I relax, putting my arms down, but I don't know how to react to this. *Should I hug her back?* I pat her gently with one hand, inhaling the soft scent of her hair as I bend closer.

Now that I think about it, I have been shown more kindness in the last rising from these little human females than I have in my entire existence. There isn't a male alive that could withstand this. No wonder all the males in my family have fallen for these small creatures. I now see why they are as protective as they are once they have them, this type of caring is rare. She lets me go on her own, and I have no idea what to say when she pats my chest right over my heart.

"Sin, I hope you find her in time. Don't forget you are not alone anymore." Then she laughs. "You know, we really need to find you a more appropriate name."

"It's the only one I have ever known. To be called something else would be a lie. However, I appreciate the thought and your kindness even though I don't deserve either, especially from you. I won't apologize for what I did then, but I will strive to take the fear out of your eyes from now on when in your presence."

"SIN, I won't lie, you have given me quite the fright several times, but you were lost. We have all been from time to time. You better go on; patience is not one of DaR's virtues. Please watch over him and the others while you're on the hunt for your female. Remember all of them have someone waiting on them back home. SiN, you're powerful alone, there is no question about that, but the ones accompanying you could be untouchable if you all work together as a team."

"I HAVE ONLY EVER HAD MYSELF."

"I KNOW, son, but you will need them if you want to succeed. She needs you more than you realize right now. There are so very few of us left now that Earth is gone. Every life is precious."

I NOD MY HEAD. She is trying to tell me something, but I never was good with hints or metaphors. I watch in envy when she runs back to Father. He picks her up, kissing her so deeply I have to look away.

· · ·

A SHARP WHISTLE gets my attention as Father motions for me to follow him. Walking briskly to his side I catch a glimpse of Kira out of the corner of my eye. A large Uana crawls up her side and onto her shoulder. Stopping dead in my tracks, I feel my fangs elongate and my shadows expand.

FATHER GRABS my arm before I can mist towards her. My mind is so focused on the animal that it takes a second for me to realize she is petting it lovingly. Father snickers beside me.

"I HAD the same reaction the first time I saw them together. Nice to know you would have defended her if need be. I bet that's messing with your mind right now, isn't it? That's Ickis, by the way. I'm sure if you think about it you have seen them together before. My Kira is the safest female on this planet because of him."

"FATHER, THEY ARE DEADLY."

"YES, this I know, but that one there. Kira has held since he was hatched and he has defended and protected her vigilantly since. XuL's mate Brittany also has one, but Iggy is not as aggressive as Ickis."

"Interesting names for such creatures."

"There is much for you to learn about our females especially if you plan on completing the bond you have already started with your own. Come, time is wasting."

Kira waves at us just as the shuttle leaves the ground. Foolishly, I find myself waving back at her like she is my best friend. The moment I see Father's grin I put my hand down feeling like a complete idiot. I have to remind myself that they are not here for me it's the female they are all trying to save. Once this mission is complete, I will just be a memory and a bad taste in their mouth. Nevertheless, I will remember her hug always.

Chapter Sixteen

SiN

I THOUGHT my small ship was impressive until we docked inside this beauty. I look around like a tourist on Targres Four, gawking at the interior as we walk its massive hallway. Artwork and intricate designs line what are usually plain spaces. Each door is even decorated with individual patterns. I can't imagine someone spending the credits or taking the time on such mundane things.

FATHER MUST HAVE NOTICED me gazing around like a youngling. "She is a beauty, isn't she?"

· · ·

"I have never seen such, even on a luxury cruiser."

"The Explorer is SoL's pride and joy. He has designed every inch of her himself. It started out as a hobby, but now it's become a passion of his. The Traveler, his other ship isn't quite as luxurious, but it can outmaneuver and outrun any other in its class."

I knew Tordan was going to be with us on the ship and this doesn't shock me, as he seldom leaves Father's side. Who I didn't expect to see was RaZ and XuL.

RaZ is sitting at the main control panel talking to SoL about the flight path. When Father and I walk into the room, all heads turn our way. The instant silence could have been cut with a knife. SoL was the first to speak up.

"Welcome aboard the Explorer. You all be good to my girl and she will take care of you. While on this mission please check out all of her amenities and let me know if there is anything that needs upgraded or added to make your stay more comfortable. I wish I was accompanying you, but as Father constantly reminds me. Someone has to stay behind to save your asses if things go bad.

. . .

"RaZ, get your grubby hands off my controls because my girl doesn't need you or your assistance. The Explorer's primary controls are linked directly to Falcor's after the last mishap with the Banhans. So, brothers take the time on board to enjoy the many little perks she provides and let someone else do the driving.

"Father, as my Alana would say. Wow, seeing you two standing side by side is quite startling. If not for your laugh lines and a few gray hairs, there would be no telling you two apart. It just dawned on me that this changes our birth number. I am no longer the third oldest. Oh well, it's of no matter, I'm still the best looking." He wags his eyebrows suggestively.

"What the frack ever, you damn giant lug head. Simply because you can beat our asses now all at once means nothing. You're just a hater because the females all flock to me and my handsome face."

"Flock boy is about right, you winged menace."

. . .

ALL THREE OF them start arguing back and forth about who is the best fighter, best looking, and so on. Their comfort in each other's company is apparent by the way they talk and threaten each other aggressively yet playfully. Once again, it proves that I am an outsider looking in.

TORDAN CLEARS HIS THROAT, "Boys, if you are all done acting like younglings, we need to get going. DaR, do we have a course to set?"

FATHER LOOKS OVER AT ME. "I can feel her, but I don't know how to get there."

SoL's massive head pops right up in front of me on a floating Holo. "Ahh, this is music to my big ears. Step forward SiN, let me introduce you to a little bit of my magic. Tordan, will you allow SiN to use your seat momentarily? SCOUT and I have been working on ways to use an alternative navigation system and SiN is going to be my first victim."

TORDAN GETS UP and motions for me to sit down. I don't know if I have ever been this uncomfortable in my life. I think I would rather be in the middle of a battlefield somewhere than confined in this room with all of them.

. . .

SoL's voice interrupts my thoughts. "SiN, the instructions are quite simple, all you need to do is lay your right hand on the pad I just lit up in front of you. The moment you do this, there will be a clear barrier drop down from the ceiling. This is nothing more than a noise cancellation device so that you can communicate directly with the ship.

"No one will be able to speak or approach you until the ship has a designated flight path. Concentrate on the person you are trying to find. However, don't be upset if this doesn't work, it's still in the development stage. Go ahead and place your palm on the pad. You will know the moment the barrier is in place, then clear your mind. Try to only focus on the human female, not any of your past flings. We don't need to be saving the wrong female."

Growling, I place my hand on the screen, ready to jerk it back the moment I feel anything, but the screen is cool to the touch. I don't have time to blink that the room goes deathly silent. Clearing my thoughts with all that's happened lately is not as easy as one may think.

. . .

Closing my eyes, the first thing that flashes through my mind is how Jade looked standing in that water, and the flash of her violet eyes when she realized she was no longer alone. The taste of her upon my lips make my mouth suddenly water. Apparently, it is her unique taste that I can remember clearer than anything else. Because it's like I suddenly have smelled my favorite meat roasting in the wind. I feel like I'm leaving my body, flying through the openness of my own mind.

For a split second, I see her with my own eyes, then it's through hers. She is weak and terrified, fighting against something or someone I can't make out clearly as she thrashes around on the bed she is tied to. I try to reach out to her, but she pushes me away and I find myself back in my own body.

My senses are immediately overwhelmed with the sounds all around me. Standing up quickly, I back away from everyone. My body misting, then solidifying as my hunger and anger start to get the best of me.

"Did you get what you need?" I can barely get the words out.

Tordan returns to his seat, and I feel the ship's engines engage. "Buckle in, I will be leaving port within the next few minutes. SoL, I need those final coordinates before we hit hyperdrive."

"ONE MOMENT, SCOUT is double-checking the readout."

"HE JUST SENT IT, SoL. Do we need to contact Commander ZoD? Since this is in his sector?"

"FATHER?"

"No, proceed. Exactly where are we headed?"

XuL ANSWERS THIS TIME. "An asteroid belt just outside the Nebula, the Destroyer is searching for other survivors in. We don't have a location yet, but there are only a few habitable planets in that quadrant. Hopefully, she will be easier to track down when we are closer. Also, there are no facilities registered in the database anywhere near those coordinates. SoL, I hope your invention doesn't have us on a wild goose chase, as my Brittany would say."

. . .

"HIS MIND WAS STRONG, and the path was clear according to SCOUT. Since it will be at least half a rotation before you arrive in that zone. Falcor will monitor your trip and notify me if need be while I step out. I have a date."

RaZ TWIRLS in his seat only stopping to ask. "You and the little lady, SoL?"

"NOPE, KEIDA."

"OHHHH, now come on. That's not fair, you do this every time we leave. You take advantage of us being away in order to keep your favorite Unka status."

"DON'T BE A HATER, RaZ, you're just jealous. Her new swords were just delivered and while everything is still quiet, this is the best time for me to take a break. She is on her way up here now. I sure am going to enjoy the hugs and brownie points I'm going to get with the two beauties I had crafted for her. She is out growing her swords as quickly as she is her clothes according to Alana."

. . .

THE MOMENT HE SAYS THAT, XuL looks up from what he is doing. "Is Danny with her?"

"No, shockingly he stayed behind this rising. Keida mentioned that because Unka Tordy wasn't on board, he was going to stay and train some with Zvranna and Raven. I don't think she cares much for that youngling female, since she snarled out her name when she was telling me about it. Keida hasn't said anything, but I think her and Danny have been spatting some.

"THE MALE IS EXTREMELY protective of her and the more aggressive her training becomes the more he is interfering. I think the younglings need a break from all the training. They are both growing up too fast and their childhood is passing by quickly. Alana reminds me constantly that they are both still kids, especially every time I give them a new weapon.

"MAYBE A FAMILY VACATION on Targres Four is in order once you return XuL. I will have Alana talk to the other females and have SAGE arrange it if they all agree. Until then, everyone, relax while you can. You have several hours before arriving at the set coordinates."

· · ·

My mind has finally settled some and I have to ask something that has been bugging me since we came on board. "Hey, I have a question while you are all here. With all this technology at your fingertips and the fact that everyone seems to be watching everything. How did the Jynrel get past you?"

Every one of them goes to laughing at the same time. Tordan seems to regain his composure the quickest, as he must have noticed I was not enjoying their humor. "DaR, would you like to tell him or me?"

Father has been standing in the middle of the room with his arms crossed, watching everything without interacting. He turns towards me, with a small smile on his face. "We allowed them to think they had found a way around our defense system. SCOUT opened up a hole and, like idiots, they slid right through. We knew after your last little stunt they would be returning for you or their credits. We had sensors following their every move. Once they landed, we could confirm that you were in the Dark Forest. We sent out drones and the moment you stepped out of Mystic. We were already moving towards you. However, I didn't anticipate the human female, nor did I expect the Jynrel to be stupid enough to attack us. At the time, you were my main concern."

· · ·

"So you used them to track me down?"

"Correct, they had ways of communicating with you that we didn't. We were also trying to find out who commissioned them to purchase human females to begin with. I'm hoping when we locate your female, we will be able to determine who is funding them. This has quickly escalated to a bigger problem than you have been up until now. Someone or something is after our mates and I am determined to find out who and why. Son's, I am going to show SiN his lodging while we are on board. I will meet you all at last meal."

He motions for me to follow him and I have to make myself remain quiet as the things floating through my head and that I want to say will not gain me any favors with any of them.

Walking a few steps behind him, I take a second to really look at the male before me. Noticing that he also wears a large cape like I do. Now I wonder, do I wear one because I have always seen him in one? Sometimes when he makes a move or a certain expression, and it's like gazing at my own face, it's disturbing.

. . .

ONLY A FEW STEPS down the hallway, he stops and one of the decorative doors opens. "This is yours while we are on the ship. SAGE set the rooms up and has also provided clothing and other needed items for your female when she comes on board."

"SHE IS NOT MY FEMALE. I haven't spoken two words to her. Just because I have this link doesn't mean she is something I want to be tied to for the rest of my life. That may have been you and the others' dream, but not mine. If I was going to pick some random female, I would have taken Melina, at least she is well-trained on how to please a male. Unlike that feral, scarred-up mess of a female this human is."

FATHER SHAKES HIS HEAD, an instant frown upon his face. "You just can't help yourself, can you? If you can't strike out at me, you are determined to do it to someone else. This female, yours or not, is your responsibility. You put her in this predicament, so you will get her out. I am sure out of all the males in this vast universe, you will not be her pick either, as you are truly a dick, as RaZ says.

"LUCKILY FOR HER, the bond is only one-sided. If we can retrieve her, we can give the female some peace and hopefully a better future than what she has experienced up to date. That's with or without you, SiN. You realize that because she is human, there are plenty that would gladly take her off your hands.

"IN YOUR ARROGANCE and need to be rid of her so quickly, I wonder how you will handle the thought of another comforting her, since you will always be able to feel her through your blood link. After all, she is just another unwanted female to you, right?"

"HOW DID YOU HANDLE IT, Father? Did it tear you to pieces the first time you felt my aunt being loved by another?"

HE GRABS me by the throat, throwing me against the wall, snarling. "You have no idea what you are saying, nor do you have the capacity to understand what you will endure if this bond is not broken. I hope she finds another, especially while you are rotting away in prison for the crimes you have committed. So that every time she reaches her peak and groans out another's name, you feel like it's ripping your very soul out.

•   •   •

"BECAUSE LET me tell you from experience, this is one thing time does not fix. In your case, the longer you are denied her, the more you will crave her. After all, you don't want her for conversation, you want her for her blood, and that's the deepest bond out there. I will only say this once and never ask me this again. It almost destroyed me and my future when I lost your aunt. However, thankfully, the Lord of Light gave me the strength to endure our separation. When he blessed me with my Kira, the bond was broken because it was replaced with something stronger."

THE MOMENT he stops talking he throws me through the doorway. Then I see a clear film close over the opening. "Oh, did I forget to tell you, welcome to your new cell even though it's much nicer than the one you just left. There is a replicator and a blood warmer in the food prep area. If you need anything else or feel something from the female, simply speak out loud and the Explorer will link you straight to me."

"THESE ROOMS WILL NOT HOLD me, Father, if I decide I want out."

"GO AHEAD and try your best, but I warn you, Danny has really enjoyed seeing how far he can push his gift. I will return when it's time. If I were you, I would relax while you can.

Your future accommodations will never be as nice as these are."

THE DOOR SHUTS and I'm suddenly alone. Looking around, even pissed. I can't help but think, *I've never even seen accommodations like these.*

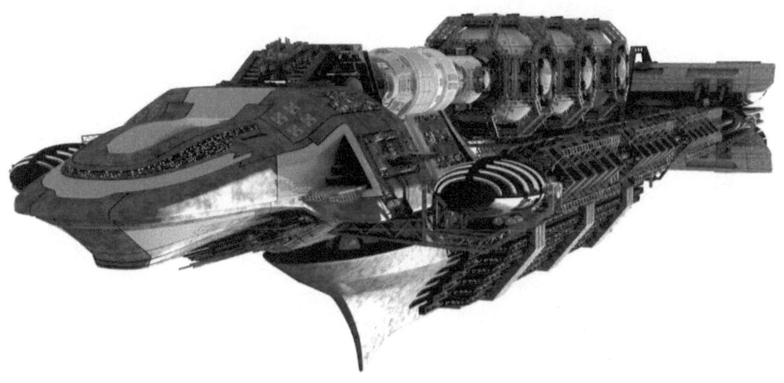

Chapter Seventeen

Jade

I MUST HAVE DONE something to upset Volten because he didn't come back this evening, nor did I get anything to eat. I have been squirming now for what feels like forever and if he doesn't come back soon, I am going to pee all over myself. Just when I don't think I can hold it any longer, the door opens, and in he strolls.

"I HAVE GOT TO PEE NOW!"

. . .

He tilts his head sideways, and all his creepy eyes focus on me like I'm the weirdo in the room. "I apologize it took a moment for my translator to understand that word. You can go ahead and relieve yourself. There is a device attached to your bed that was designed to catch all body fluids."

"What, am I just supposed to pee on myself?"

"There will be no mess. After you are finished, simply hit the blue button on your right and an Ionizer will run along your skin. Cleaning the bedding, clothing, and your body all simultaneously."

"You could have informed me of this before you took off yesterday, and thanks for the food by the way. My stomach thinks my throat has been cut I'm so hungry."

"I didn't forget your substance deliberately, but your blood test came back inconclusive and I thought that possibly it was because of what you had eaten that rising. I'm going to retake the samples again and hopefully the results will be clearer this time."

. . .

I SHY AWAY from him as he moves closer, with a huge needle in one of his many hands.

"YOU HAVE no reason to be alarmed, Jade. However, the sample needs to be obtained from a pure source and this could be slightly uncomfortable for you. Because I don't want you to be stressed unnecessarily. I am going to mildly sedate you, try to relax, and we will have this over with shortly."

HE DOESN'T EVEN GIVE me a second to say no before I start seeing those damn bubbles again. Then I'm mortified when I feel my bladder release. My mind immediately clears itself of the sedative when a sharp piercing pain on the inside of my thigh has me screaming out. Instinctively, I start fighting against the restraints. For a split second, I swear I see SiN standing at the foot of the bed. Until a heavy fog falls over my mind and I feel myself floating away as everything goes dark.

WHEN I OPEN my eyes again, I find myself standing in that creek again with the weird white water. Everything looks fuzzy around me, but I recognize his growl immediately. It's like déjà vu all over again. Moving in slow motion, I relive the first moment I saw him awake. This time seems the same, but different, almost dreamlike. When I was treating SiN's wounds, I made up my own version of what his personality would be, now it's like I'm living out my fantasy.

HE STANDS before me breathing heavily and all this does is enhance the intricate lines and dips that flow across his naked body. Even coated in my blood and burned skin, he takes my breath away. If there is a flaw on him I have yet to find it. Now that he is awake, I can see the fire that dances behind those intense yellow eyes of his. When he steps towards me, I can't help but notice his shaft slowly hardening with each step.

BEFORE I CAN BLINK, he is holding me in his arms, but this time it's not in anger like before. Instead, he pulls me to him, gently nuzzling my neck as he whispers soft, soothing words I can't make out clearly.

MY BODY instantly reacts to his wondering hands as my nipples harden against his naked chest. He grinds his shaft against my lower stomach, and I whimper as he explores me thoroughly. Massive hands roam my body freely as he kisses and nips my neck. A sharp pain has me crying out, only for desire, unlike anything I have ever known rushes through me. I can barely hold on to him as my body responds to all this stimulation.

· · ·

I CAN FEEL myself getting frailer, with each pull on my neck. Despite knowing I should say something, I don't want this to end. I've never been held in such a way or felt this wanted and desired. How long has it been since someone held me this tenderly? I have no way of knowing, but I feel like this is a first for me.

THE STRENGTH of his body against mine is so vast that I can physically feel power pulsing beneath his skin. His body twitches, and I swear he is getting larger. His body surrounds me completely as he clutches me to him like I mean something.

HE PULLS one of my legs up, hooking it around his waist as he rubs his shaft against my damp folds. My inner thighs already wet from my own desire. I crave him like no other even as I feel myself getting weaker the longer he takes deep pulls from my neck. I want him to take it all if it means he will continue to embrace me like this.

PULLING AWAY, he holds me slightly away from him as he peers deeply into my eyes. My blood starts to drip down his chin, but a wicked long tongue swipes it up before it can drip away. Piercing yellow eyes caress my skin as he gazes at me like I'm something special. When his mouth crashes onto mine, I must have been holding my breath because when I part my lips to take a breath, he invades mine. Our tongues duel together as his hands grip me almost painfully. Thrusting his shaft into me all at once. I scream out in pleasure and pain as he rolls his hips, giving me time to adjust to his immense size.

HE SEEMS to lose all control after that. Ravaging my neck and breast, biting me over and over in this sexual frenzy we have created together. His wild thrust bounces me around like a rag doll. One last hard pull from my breast and I feel him reach his own peak as his shaft pulses his hot seed inside of me. He slowly pulls out of me before lowering us both to the ground, kissing me gently on the forehead as he gets up. This is when I notice a large pool of blood gathering underneath my body. I reach out for him, but it's like he no longer sees me.

SIN TURNS FROM ME, and I watch as he washes himself off in the creek I had been standing in earlier. Once free of the blood and our combined fluids, he steps out. He doesn't even look back at me, just walks away into the darkness of the forest surrounding us. For a moment, he appears again from another location, but something is different with this ghost-like appearance. Then, everything begins to fade.

· · ·

My heart starts beating hard in my chest as the wetness of my own blood seeps into the ground around me. Confused and weak, I no longer have any fight left in me, so I let go, hoping that death finally takes me. Only for my eyes to open back up in that room again. There is blood on the sheets around the top of my legs as I lay here naked for all to see, but other than that, I seem to be fine. The sound of a voice beside me has me screaming out.

"You're fine Jade, no reason for hysterics. That was quite an interesting dream you were having there. Who is this male that seems to be haunting you?"

"That wasn't real?" I ask out loud as my mind wonders how he knew I was dreaming.

"No, it wasn't real, but you were very vocal, and your readings were elevated. The sedative I gave you tends to bring on hallucinations. Your species' bodies react quickly to it and the results are usually always the same. Every female that has been given this substance wakes up screaming the same as you did."

. . .

"Volten, you have to be mistaken. I could feel his hands on my body, the warmth of my own blood running down my chest."

"The brain is a powerful thing, Jade. Now that you are awake, I will commence in cleaning you up. The moment I inserted the needle you reacted violently, spewing your precious blood everywhere. Giving me no choice but to sedate you heavier.

"I will provide you with substance momentarily since I was finally able to get a clean sample of your blood. It appears that your blood is indeed poisonous, just not to my species. You are the carrier of the deadly virus we were looking for, but you are not affected by it at all. We still have much to learn about your kind, especially since not all of your species carries this genetic trait. The good news is it makes you valuable to them. They will provide better treatment and meals for you as long as your body holds up."

"What do you mean, my body holds up?"

"Each rising, I will come back and remove as much blood as possible from you. This will be very stressful on your delicate system and will weaken your heart quicker than normal. It should please you to know that every drop will be used in the defense of my superiors' race. Unfortunately, because your race is so small, you will not be able to provide all that is required, and now the hunt for others of your kind has been elevated. It will take several of you to provide the adequate amounts needed for this to be successful."

"So, in other words, you will use me until my heart gives out. Humans can reproduce the blood that we need, but we didn't come with a huge amount of extra."

"Jade, I will have to monitor you constantly. For your own good, you need to eat everything I bring you. We will provide reading and entertainment for you to keep your mind stimulated. You'll also have access to the exercise facility and the gardens as long as you remain compliant. I will do my best to try and keep your spirits up and make your time here as pleasant as possible, Jade."

"What happens to the ones you catch that don't have this virus you're talking about?"

"They will be disposed of or used in another fashion."

. . .

I LAY my head back and close my eyes, rewinding everything that's happened to me since I woke up in that damn cage. "Seems like everyone wants something from me and they all lead to my death." The moment I say that, I realize how true those words are. This is my body and I refuse to let them use me for some type of biowarfare. The moment Volten leaves I will find a way to end this. Either by my own hand or another's. Just once, I would love to be in control of my existence. I'm tired of being mistreated and hurt for the pleasure of others.

FOR A SECOND, I allow myself to replay the so-called dream I just had. How wonderful would it be to be loved like that for real?

Chapter Eighteen

SiN

PACING AROUND THIS GLORIFIED CELL, it takes all I have not to try to escape. The fact that we are in the middle of space and the only other ship on board happens to be a short-distance shuttle, is the one thing holding me here at this moment.

I KNOW things are going to get much worse for me. I can't believe I allowed myself to get caught, or that I didn't see through my mother's lies. Falling back onto the bed, I stare up at the decorative ceiling and shake my head at the unseen amount of credits wasted on this ship.

· · ·

THROWING my arm over my eyes, I think back through the last few risings and the events that led me here. What could I have done differently? How did my decisions lead me to this? I have always been steps ahead of them and now I feel like I'm in limbo. This constant craving is driving me crazy. It's like no matter what I eat, it never hits the spot. I hate being out of control.

SLEEP SEEMS to be pulling at me, with nothing else to do, I let my mind relax. I need to find a way out of this mess and away from my father. I have to be ready to run on a moment's notice. At least my ship is still safe, and I have enough credits stored on board to relocate somewhere else, but where?

IT'S NOT like I blend in easily with this face. The moment I run, they will have every bounty hunter in the region searching for me. This new eating disorder is not going to help matters either if I don't find something else to sustain me. There has to be a way to reverse craving this once I get out of here. Perhaps I will ask one of the priestesses on Xuias. If anyone has the answer, or a cure, it would be one of them.

I MUST HAVE DRIFTED off to sleep because the next thing I know, I'm having a very interesting dream, or possibly a fantasy, about the little human female. I'm holding her tenderly against my naked chest. Two lines of red blood run down her neck and my eyes follow as it curves around her lovely breasts, beckoning me to taste them. The moment I start to lick the blood from her pale skin. I feel a rush of power pulse beneath my skin, unlike anything I have ever experienced. My body twitches, and I swear I feel like I'm getting larger. Is her blood giving me this rush of energy? My mind becomes muddled and confused the more of her I ingest. No matter how much I lick or pull from her I want more. I can't seem to get close enough.

GRABBING HER LEGS, I hook them around my waist. Rubbing my shaft against her damp folds with one hand, while I grip her fleshly ass with the other. I realize quickly that I'm powerless when it comes to her. This high is only something she can provide and if there was a way for me to consume her whole, I know there would be no stopping me.

SHE TREMBLES IN MY ARMS, but I can feel and smell her desire. I have no words of comfort for her as I slam into her damp folds. My hard thrust bounce her small body aggressive and relentless as I hold her tight in my arms Her walls milk me of all thought as I latch back onto her neck. Pulling her unique taste into my mouth as my body continues to crave more. In a frenzy, I lose complete control, rutting her like an untried youth seeking only my release with no care for the female.

. . .

I ROAR out as one of the strongest releases of my life flows through me. My body now strumming with unreleased power. The instant my mind clears, I realize I have done exactly what they wanted. Once I had tasted the pleasure of her flesh, they knew I would immediately want and crave more. *I will prove them all wrong, no one will control me, not even something as delicious as her.*

AGGRESSIVELY, I pull out of her and throw her to the ground, a snarl on my lips as I have no way of knowing her role in this game we play. She curls into a ball and tears flow from her eyes. She appears small and broken, lying there. What's left of her blood pools around her on the ground. I almost reach down to pull her back into my arms, but I make myself resist. If she is no longer around, then the temptation and the bond will be broken.

THE SOUND of my laughter echoes around us. Oddly now, it's like I am suddenly standing back watching myself and the female from another angle. *What the frack?* I go from an awesome wet dream to this. *Where the frack am I?*

. . .

"YOU NOR ANY other will hold me captive ... bond or not human. They thought they could use you as a way to control me, but they should have known that I would find a way out. Sorry, it had to end this way, little female, but you are a bond I am not willing to endure for life. May the gods take you quickly and hopefully your next life will be kinder to you than this one has been."

I WATCH myself wash off in the creek like I don't have a care in the world. The female cries pitifully on the ground, her body used and thrown away like trash, and it actually angers me. Is this who I am or who I've always been? All about myself with no thought or care for others. I step forward and her eyes turn towards me confused. She glances back towards the forest, then back toward me. Closing her eyes, she fades away right in front of me.

IMMEDIATELY, I run over to where she is only to find myself in the shadows of another location. A Chilten is standing over her as she fights against the restraints holding her to a bed. Neither of them seem to notice me here.

IT TAKES me a moment to realize that this is where I saw her originally when we were trying to find a flight path, but at the time I didn't realize she was naked lying there. Now I can barely take my eyes off her. The first time I saw her in that creek I was angry and full of rage. Now that I've had time to see the situation for what it was, either in a dream or reality. I have experienced the taste and feel of her, I no longer see her the same.

THE SCARS DON'T TAKE away from her beauty. If anything, they simply prove her strength and will to survive. From this angle, I can see all the dips and curves of her small body. Even now, I can still feel her soft skin under my fingertips. Her face I feel like I have gazed upon my whole life. The pull I feel towards her makes me uncomfortable. In my mind, there is no way simply tasting someone could link us together like this, but I feel her inside of me.

I CAN TELL they are talking about something that is upsetting her just by the emotions on her face. No matter how hard I try, I can't make out their words. I feel like a ghost in the room. At one point, she even looks straight at me, but her eyes never meet mine. I don't know where I am or how I got here, but something tells me to pay attention. Walking around the room, I watch each and every thing he is doing to her. After a little while, I see her restraints release, and she sits up on the bed.

. . .

THE CHILTEN HANDS her some sort of covering and a tray appears on a table on the other side of her bed. It takes her a moment to get off the bed and I can tell the moment she steps down she is struggling. She seems overly pale and weak like her life force is being drained out of her.

LORD OF LIGHT, that's exactly what is happening here. The clues are everywhere she is being held and tested in some sort of facility. The Jynrel told me they were purchasing the females for testing, and I never questioned it. What is it about these females that makes them so valuable? Drops of her red blood cover the blanket she was lying on. A machine comes out of the ceiling and cleans the bedding while I watch her struggle to eat the substance she was given.

SHE IS HUNCHED OVER, almost wilting in on herself. The Chilten is not watching her like I am. So, he doesn't see her slip the utensil she was eating with into the sleeve of the robe-like thing he gave her to cover herself.

HE SAYS something to her then the door opens. After a brief moment of hesitation, I decide to follow him out. I need to find out as much as I can about this place if we are going to have any chance of saving her.

. . .

I JUMP from shadow to shadow, keeping to the darkness and the corners just in case someone can actually see me. He stops multiple times, talking to others of his kind. Several other doors open and close, giving me seconds to glance inside. There seem to be females of every race enclosed behind all these multiple doors. All of them contained and dressed in the same manner.

WHAT ARE YOU LOOKING FOR? I whisper out, not expecting an answer.

A scream echoes through the hallway and I turn just in time to see another human female running towards me. Long blond hair tangles around her face and upper arms as she turns her head frantically looking for a way out. She runs right past me, but the sight of a huge white arm grabbing her stops me from getting any closer.

THE FEMALE STRUGGLES against his hold, but there will be no escaping for her. Not against him, the one male I would have never dreamed would be in a place like this. Commander ZoD. Even though we are close in height, his body is a solid mass of muscles on top of muscles; the male is massive. It's a battle I am not sure I could win even though Father defeated him multiple times in the Commander trials. He pulls the struggling female near, saying something to her and she spits in his face.

. . .

I LOOK AROUND, trying to find a way to distract him without revealing myself. Because I know he is going to kill her for that. When suddenly I hear him start laughing, I am almost relieved. Only to be shocked further at how violent the tiny little female gets as she struggles to get loose. He simply tosses her over his shoulder and walks away. Her vocabulary becomes even more colorful as she beats her small hands against his back.

I START TO FOLLOW THEM, but I don't want to get sidetracked or too far from my own female. That thought stops me in my tracks for a second. I can't allow myself to think about her like that. If I call her by her name, it makes all of this too real. I have to find a way to get her out of here, a way for me to escape in the mix. There has to be a shuttle entrance or a side port where supplies are usually delivered somewhere around here.

I HAD JUST STEPPED into the hallway when I hear someone shout out my name.

Chapter Nineteen

DaR

I HAVE SPENT the last part of this rising, going over the charges the elders have placed on SiN. The list seems non-ending with the offenses he is being accused of. Aggravated, and needing someone to talk to. I reach over and hit the comm button.

EVERY TIME my father's face appears on the screen, I'm shocked and joyful. I spent many risings I without the luxury of having him to talk to. "DaR, Victoria just spoke to Kira. You should have notified me sooner that you were leaving."

. . .

"THINGS PROGRESSED QUICKLY, and someone needed to stay behind. I knew between you and SoL the females would remain safe. Have you had time to look over the charges that have been presented to the elders?"

"I TAKE it you still have him in custody?"

"YES, YOU SEEM SHOCKED BY THAT."

"HE HASN'T BEEN EASILY CAUGHT up to date, so I simply figured holding him would prove just as difficult."

"THAT'S one of the reasons I left immediately. There is no way for him to physically leave this ship until we land. Looking upon him hurts my heart, Father." I throw the papers down and run a hand through my hair, closing my eyes for a moment. "Since the moment I took on the responsibility of Darverius and then the births of my sons, I have strived to do right by them all. When I look at this list, I don't see his failures, I see my own.

"HOW DID I NOT KNOW? I have questioned myself multiple times from the moment I learned of him and Ellaria. I had a daughter, my mind can't even grasp that. Now from what I understand, she has disappeared. Gone, before I could even comprehend I had her. I wasted time with insignificant things instead of searching her out in the Dark Forest and now, it seems I have lost my chance. I'm torn, the Commander in me believes he should rot away in a faraway prison for what he has done. The Father in me is trying to find a way to save him."

"DaR you are beating yourself up for something that was out of your control. You know as well as I do we all have free will. He knew what he was doing was wrong and that others might be hurt or killed. He is not a youngling who does not know right from wrong he is a grown male who knew better. You can blame the who and what's that raised him all you want, but they didn't do the deeds … he did. If anyone has paid for his misdeeds, it's been you, son. Just how many of his crimes did you take as your own?"

"More than I should have. I simply feel like I have failed him. I watch him struggle to be around my other sons, and I try to put myself in his place. They have always had each other, while he has been alone. He has no idea how to interact with them, so he simply strikes out. I wonder if he will ever truly be comfortable or accepted by them.

. . .

"BEFORE WE LEFT, Katherine showed him something that has given him pause, but even I can tell that's not going to last. Not the way everyone is on edge around him. I questioned Katherine afterward, but she refused to tell me. She said it was his story to tell, but the odds of him ever opening up to me are slim.

"HE DID SPEAK to Kira with respect and tenderness, which shocked me as many times she has been his primary target to get to me. I didn't know he was even capable of having a normal conversation until he spoke with her. SiN is spontaneous, willful, and domineering. Definitely not a team player, but he also wears his heart on his sleeve. Kira saw it before any of us did. She told me he was acting out because he knew no other way to get my attention. I really didn't know how to react when he waved to her like a youngling when we were leaving.

"EVEN IF BY some miracle we are able to redeem him somehow, he will never fully fit in. He is not a follower, he is a leader and that alone would make him butt heads with the others."

"DAR, in the mix of all this. I wasn't going to bring up the conversation I heard between Victoria and Kira earlier, but

Kira brought up a very valid point. What if SiN is not the only one you knew nothing about?"

FATHER HOLDS UP HIS HAND, stopping me before I can say anything. "You are well aware of what SoL's mother did to conceive him. What makes you think that others could not have done the same? SiN's mother was demented, and SoL's mother was desperate, but they still succeeded. SoL and you both were lucky that someone recognized the symbol on his arm. As big as that male is, he could have turned out to be worse than SiN did. SiN forged your House mark, when he could have been tested and it would have been granted to him. He knew he was tied to you, and he simply found ways to manipulate that knowledge. Another may not know of you at all."

"I CAN'T EVEN THINK about that, all I can do is pray that this is the last of the unknowns. My boys are just a big a handful grown now, as they were as younglings. I am proud of the fact that most of them are living their own lives and building their fortunes with little to no help from me. SiN just seems so different from the others."

.   .   .

"DaR, it's because you see yourself in more than just his skin. You see, the male you could have easily become if your choices had been different."

"You're probably right, Father. We are headed into the outer sector, and I have a feeling things are going to get interesting once we get there. I hate heading into the unknown."

"Did you contact ZoD and let him know you were entering the area?"

"No, my gut tells me he is involved in this some way. Especially after our last conversation. He is hiding something and after this is over, I plan on finding out exactly what that is."

The evening dinner bell ringing interrupts us. "DaR, you go on, keep those boys and yourself safe out there." Putting his hand across his chest he says the words I have always tried to live by. "Strength and honor, my son."

"Strength and honor, my father."

·   ·   ·

THE SCREEN GOES BLACK, and I run a weary hand through my hair. I almost comm Kira just to see her face, but instead, I make myself get up. Strolling down the hallway, I can't help but look at the overabundance of luxuries SoL has done to this ship. Who would have thought one of the biggest males in this known universe would have such decorating skills?

OPENING SiN's DOOR, I walk in only to find him draped across the sleeping platform. Using my foot, I nudge him to get up, only for my foot to pass right through him. "What the frack?"

SHOCKED, I reach down only for my hands to do the same thing. "Explorer, tell RaZ and XuL I need them! I need them to report here immediately!"

"CONFIRMED, COMMANDER."

SiN DOESN'T MOVE AT ALL. I can't even tell if he is breathing, but something odd is happening to his right arm. The small ring of Symbots that had left me and merged into him are moving. Unlike mine, which normally covers my skin completely, his is taking on a pattern. Oddly enough, it looks like a tree root. My house symbol that he had forged is slowly disappearing right before my eyes. What is going on with this male?

I FEEL the brush of RaZ's wings just as he enters the doorway. "What the frack, did the dumbass forget to eat?"

"THIS DOESN'T LOOK like a death sleep to me, RaZ." XuL quickly replies as he goes to the other side of the sleeping platform. I watch as his hands also pass through SiN's body.

RaZ JUMPS BACK. "Ok, that's some freaky shit right there. Is this part of the mist thing that he does?"

"I HAVE NO CLUE. The few times I have seen him mist away he appears as thick fog. This is different it's like he is here but gone at the same time."

XuL STEPS back away from the platform. "Call grandfather."

I HIT THE COMM UNIT. The moment father appears on the screen I could see the instant concern on his face. "DaR what's wrong; are you all safe?"

. . .

"YES, and no ... or maybe, I should say we have no clue. Hold on, let me show you what I mean. Explorer, open the interior feed for this room and connect it to this comms location." Moments later, father appears upon a floating Holo screen. I point towards SiN.

"HE LOOKS like he is asleep and just walking by you would never know ... this." When my hand passes through him, Father looks just as shocked.

"I HAVE NEVER WITNESSED anything like this, Father. It's like he is a phantom, or ghost."

WHEN HE SAYS THIS, my first thoughts are of Ellaria. "Wait a minute, that just may be the answer. Do you think he might have obtained the same powers Ellaria had? They were twins after all and she would simply pop into existence, looking very similar to ... this."

FATHER SHAKES HIS HEAD NO. "DaR, Ellaria was a force of unknown origin and power. I have searched through archives looking for anything similar to her with no success. I am not sure we will ever truly understand how she remained here or the power she welded. They shared the same essence, this could be another trait that has lay dormant passed from parent to child. There were rumors of elders who could project themselves in the early days of Darverius, but it's not something I have ever witnessed myself. Wait a minute, SCOUT, are you listening?"

"I am."

"Can you help us out here?"

"I have scanned his body and if my calculations are right, the term of what is occurring, is called, Astral projection. If the archives are correct, he is currently elsewhere, even though his mass is still here. This was a common trait when the elders first relocated to Darverius, but as time continued, it was used less and less. So, the gene became dormant."

"DaR, on Earth we were able to flash from one location to another with a simple thought. All I had to do was think of the location and I was there. RaZ saw this firsthand, and it was one of the hardest things for Katherine and Victoria to get used to when we came back to Darverius. We could no longer manipulate our bodies in that way. If the elders' genes have reawakened and this is a form of Astral Projection, that means he can be in two places at once. With training and enough practice, he could interact successfully in both forms, and no one would be the wiser. If imprisoned, this will make it extremely hard to contain him completely."

RaZ's WINGS twitch behind him as he backs further away from SiN. "Let me get this straight. If I had this, I could be in a meeting and home both simultaneously. Why do the freaks get all the cool stuff? Basically, what you're telling us, Grandfather, is that Mist boy here now has some sort of superpower where he can leave his body and go floating around somewhere else. That's just creepy as shit. His mist thing was bad enough. Someone needs to file a complaint with the superpower gods and let them know this crazy fucker has enough issues without this."

"MASTER RaZ, my thoughts on this are as follows. He doesn't even know he is somewhere else, especially if this is the first time this has occurred. You have had him in concentrating on the bond he has with Mistress Jade. By the location of his body, he simply laid down and probably believes he is dreaming."

. . .

"So, SCOUT, your mega brain thinks he is just in Lala land?"

"Well said, Master RaZ."

"How do we get him back here?"

"Have you tried calling out to him?"

Everyone looks at me. "Ahhh, no."

"I would probably start there, Commander."

Everyone tries to hide their laughter and I even see Father shake his head on the Holo screen in amusement. However, my temper is slowly rising. "SCOUT, that wasn't the sound of sarcasm coming from you was it."

"I was simply making a suggestion Commander, after all, you did call me."

. . .

"No wonder I have frackin gray hairs. SiN, get the frack up!" I scream out.

When he doesn't move, all of us say his name at once. He jerks straight up onto his feet, arms stretched out ready to fight.

"What the frack are you all doing in here? Can't a male rest in his own prison without interruptions?"

"Is that what you were doing SiN, resting?"

He lowers his arms down, relaxing some, but not before he notices the black markings on his arm. He points at it, then me. "What's this?"

I just shrug my shoulders, "I don't have a clue."

"Well, I wish the hell someone knew what was going on with me. I feel like I was just dropped into this body, and what the frack do you mean … Is that what you were doing? It's not like I can get out of this pretty cage of yours."

.   .   .

"ARE YOU CERTAIN OF THAT, SiN? Because I'm not sure you were here resting. I believe you we're somewhere else?"

SUDDENLY HE HAS a puzzled look on his face. "How to answer that? I mean, I think, I was dreaming of pieces of it. Then things changed, and I found myself in a room. Wait, I think I may have seen the facility they are holding the female in, and she is not the only one there either. They had chambers full of different species."

"WHILE YOU WERE GAZING AT ALL the females, did you find out anything useful, Mist boy?"

"YOU WINGED PRICK, one of these risings."

"YEAH, yeah, Mist boy. Bring it on, anytime."

SiN LAUNCHES at RaZ and I barely grab him in time. "That's enough, both of you are acting like younglings. You two need to put your petty differences aside, we have a female to rescue here. I don't care if you two beat the ever-loving frack out of each other when we get back, but you both are on my last nerve, and that's not a good place to be right now."

A voice suddenly interrupts us. "Commander, Tordan wanted me to inform you that we are approaching the outer corridor. If you are planning on consuming your last meal, you should proceed."

"Thank you, Explorer … Do you all think you could act civil for a few moments?"

Xul holds his hands up. "Don't include me in their mess. I just want the opportunity to watch."

Father laughing as he has watched all of this from the Holo screen in the background is the last thing I hear as I walk out the door toward the food prep area. "I need a vacation."

Chapter Twenty

SiN

MY FANCY PRISON door opens and I see the clear force field drop. I don't even get up from the chair I have been lounging in. My mind is still trying to sort through all the things that have happened in the last couple of risings.

UNCONSCIOUSLY, I keep rubbing my arm where this strange marking has appeared under my skin. At first glance, I thought something had grown up it, but the skin is smooth to the touch. Just one more weird thing to add to the list of all the new things happening to my body. It's so frustrating. I have spent my entire life learning how to use my differences to my advantage. Now I feel like a youngling all over again.

WE MUST BE GETTING close to the female because her feelings have become clearer. I still have no idea how I managed to find myself in that facility with her, or if I can do it again.

"MASTER SIN, your presence is needed on the control deck."

I GROWL as I get up. I know if I don't go on my own, they'll just come get me. What I am shocked of though, is no one is waiting in the hallway for me. I stand there for a moment contemplating whether to do what I'm told or take my chances with the shuttle now that we are closer to the planets.

EVEN THOUGH I may kick myself in the ass for this later. I turn and walk towards the control room. Upon entering, Father is in his normal spot, standing in the middle of the room, watching everything with his arms crossed. The viewer shows us nearing an asteroid belt on the outside of the largest Nebula I have ever seen. The ship suddenly halts in dead space, and I stumble slightly. I notice Father doesn't even move, of course.

. . .

AN UNMARKED CRUISER leaving a small asteroid directly in front of the viewer barely misses us as it hits hyperspace.

"WHOOOO, frack that was close. Who is driving this bucket of bolts? That was some impressive reaction time right there."

"THANK YOU, Master SiN, I appreciate your compliment. My scanners picked up the other vessel entering our direct flight path, and I only had a moment to maneuver us into a better location, as the other vehicle could not see us as we were still cloaked at this time. I do apologize if I startled you."

I GLANCE over at Father and then at the others, looking at different screens on the control panels in front of them. "SiN, say hello to the Explorer. She is new to the fleet and her sentient programming is still in its early stage, but she is learning quickly."

"HELLO, Explorer I will say if your exterior looks anything like the interior, you are quite the beauty."

"ACKNOWLEDGED, MASTER SiN."

. . .

I SEE RaZ roll his eyes, but before I can say anything XuL turns his attention to me. "SiN, when you took your little trip. Were there any landmarks or anything that stood out about the facility? Something that might give us some insights to what we're dealing with?"

"IT WAS some sort of medical place. If I got back inside, I believe I could figure out where they are holding the female quickly, but I couldn't understand a word they were saying."

TORDAN TURNS AROUND, "Who was saying? You didn't tell us you saw anyone besides the females."

"I WAS TOO busy getting drilled about leaving in the first place, if you all recall."

WHEN XuL's eyes flash black and some of his runes start to move on his skin, I step back. "SiN, you need to start from the beginning." He practically snarls out.

"FRACK you all need to lighten up some, I am fracking tired of being on the defense with all of you nonstop. All I know is, I appeared next to the female. She was strapped to a table, a bed-like thing. There was a Chilten standing over her. It looked like he had just removed a needle from the inside of her leg, because there was blood on her legs. She was laying there naked, shivering, and covered in bruises. He continued to poke and probe at her. When he left, I was torn about staying with her or following him, but I knew I needed to see what they were doing.

"SEVERAL OF THOSE Chilten were walking in and out of the rooms. I couldn't understand a single thing they were saying to each other. I was getting ready to head back towards the female. When another human female with different coloring came running straight at me. She was only a few steps away when she was captured by another. Father, this information you will find quite interesting.

"IT WAS COMMANDER ZOD. He grabbed the female just as she was approaching me. I was standing right in front of her and she never acknowledged me. She fought him like a baby Suet even after he threw her over his shoulder. The one thing I did notice in this place was one long hallway after another. There has to be hundreds of chambers inside."

. . .

ALL EYES WERE upon me as I finished my story. Father looks like he was ready to tear this ship apart with his bare hands. His runes pulsing with his anger.

SCOUT's VOICE interrupts any other questions they were going to throw at me. "Commander DaR, I may have a solution."

"GO AHEAD, SCOUT."

BEFORE I HAVE time to react, a large mountain of a male is standing directly in front of me looking down. "Woah, where the frack did you come from? And big guy, some personal space here. I would advise you to step back and get out of my face."

HE ACTUALLY STEPS CLOSER his fist clenching and the veins pulse in his neck with his anger. There is no missing this male wants to wipe the floor with me and until Father speaks up, I don't understand his anger.

.   .   .

"SCOUT, what are you doing here? You know I am not comfortable with you appearing in your solid form after the last incident."

"Commander, I have taken precautions, and I can guarantee that will never happen again no matter the circumstances. I believe I can shorten the amount of time it's going to take in order to locate the facility that is holding Mistress Jade. That is, if Master SiN here is willing to participate."

"Yeah, I don't think we are going to play well together SCOUT. Maybe you should pick someone else for your little experiment."

"Let it be said, you of all males are not my favorite. However, I am not here for you. I am here for Mistress Jade, and you are the only one who can pull this off." He holds a small device in his hand.

"What is that, a mini bomb that's meant to blow my head off when I step out of line?"

. . .

"No, but I suppose I could work on that next. This is a transponder that I have reprogramed as a locator. However, I have a question before we proceed. When you projected yourself, you were fully clothed, correct?"

"Yeah, I believe so, but wouldn't the device just show that I was still on this ship?"

"This one has been modified, like I said. If my calculations are accurate, it will show you in both locations simultaneously. Mistress Jade has been there long enough already and from what you said she is being mistreated. Are you ready to take a nap?" His fist tightens over the device as he glares down at me.

"Me and you are never going to be friends, are we big guy?"

"I would say your words are most accurate."

Xul motions for all of us to come to him. I step around SCOUT and approach hesitantly, not comfortable with this guy at my back. "I wanted you all to see this, there is a belt of asteroids in this area right here. All of them have some sort of gravitational pull holding them in place. Unlike the others in this area, that are getting slowly pulled into the Nebula.

"That facility has to be on one of these, but the moment we are spotted they will more than likely destroy the facility. The Nebula is putting off small solar storms in this area, and they may be the only way for us to approach without alerting them. If they are holding that many females in this area, we can't take the chance of them blowing the place. I commed the Destroyer, but EvO has not responded. I was hoping they were close to our coordinates in case we needed help with the evacuation."

Tordan speaks up. "The Explorer can hold a significant amount, but there are just so many unknowns. SiN, if you could get back in there, it would be a great help. We are flying blind here."

Looking at all of them, I shrug. "I'm not saying I won't do it. I simply have no idea how I did it to begin with."

RaZ bumps my shoulder with his wing. "What were you thinking about when you laid down earlier, Mist boy?"

. . .

"KICKING YOUR WINGED ASS."

"THAT'S ENOUGH! One more word out of either of you, or I swear all that will be left to return to your mates, will be pieces in a smashed up box. SiN answer the frackin question."

"FRACK, I don't know, and no amount of yelling at me is going to make it happen, either. I was probably thinking all the crap that's happened in the last couple of risings. I was damn near burned in half, then Mystic, Ellaria, my mother, let's not forget the reason why we are all here, the little female, or that I was locked up in a glorified cage. What answer do you want? I fell asleep, or I think I did, and the next thing I knew I was there."

"COMMANDER, if I may. I believe I can hurry this along."

"BE MY GUEST, SCOUT."

"MASTER SiN, I need you to attach this to your belt."

. . .

I TAKE the small device from him and clip it on. Before I even see him move, I feel myself crumbling to the floor. In the next heartbeat, I find myself standing back in the hallway of the facility.

DaR

I barely catch SiN's body before he hits the floor. Picking his large frame up in my arms. I turn towards SCOUT, who the moment sees my face wipes the smirk off his face.

"WHAT HAVE you done to him, SCOUT?"

"NOTHING PERMANENT, Commander, I simply pressed a nerve that rendered him unconscious. He will regain consciousness shortly. There was no time left for him to do this naturally."

"HOW DO you even know it will work just because he is out? The last time, his body only appeared solid."

. . .

"FATHER, I'M GETTING A READING," XuL yells out. Then Tordan starts barking orders. "Explorer, I need you to lock onto SiN's location, but remain cloaked."

"CONFIRMED."

ADJUSTING SiN IN MY ARMS, I turn, heading towards his rooms so I can lay him down. SCOUT follows slightly behind me. "You know SCOUT you could have waited until he was sitting down, or even back in his rooms. He is not exactly light."

"PERHAPS."

"YOU SEEM to be enjoy him crumbling in front of you a little too much."

"JUST WANTED the male to get an understanding of what it feels like to have no control."

. . .

"I RECKON HE DESERVED THAT. I will allow you this one time revenge because of what he did to you, but let it be logged, SCOUT. No further actions against him will be tolerated."

"IT HAS BEEN RECORDED. It's against my programming to go against a direct order."

GETTING both of our large frames through the doorway takes me a couple of tries. "I am getting too old to keep toting my sons around like they are younglings," I mumble to myself as I lay him down.

PULLING UP A CHAIR, I sit there wearily, missing My Kira and her comforting arms. When this mission is done, I'm going to take her somewhere we can be alone for rotations.

SCOUT's VOICE pulls me out of my thoughts. "Commander, I have now uplinked to the facility and I am in the process of downloading it's schematics now. I will be quiet for a few moments until it's completed. I'm also able to track Master SiN as he moves through the facility now."

Chapter Twenty-One

SiN

FINDING myself back where I was, I immediately turn towards the little female. My legs not allowing me to go in any other direction until I can see that she is safe. The door slides open as I approach, and I look around to see if anyone notices. Her room is dark, but that doesn't make any difference to me as my vision adjusts quickly.

SHE LAY there strapped back to the bed again, with dried tear marks lining her cheeks. When I reach up to touch her face, my hand passes right through her. She looks so tiny lying here. She stirs for a moment, opening sleepy violet eyes. Glancing around, I realize quickly that she can't see me. A shiver wracks her small frame and I'm instantly angered that I can't pull the covers up on her.

SHE CLOSES HER EYES, but her words stop me dead in my tracks as I turn to leave the room. "Please, God, I don't know what I have done to deserve this, but I pray you give me the strength to end it. I pray that you take me into your arms and that I'm worthy enough to be granted the peace I have always prayed for. I've tried to be strong, but I have no more to give. Forgive me for what I am about to do, but I won't let them use me, to harm others. Tomorrow, all this will finally end and the only thing I regret is … well you already know this … but for once, it would have been nice to be wanted."

I FEEL her sorrow and acceptance that this is the end for her like it's my own. I don't know how to tell her I'm coming, and not to give up, but it's like she has pushed me out of her mind.

THIS TIME when I try to touch her, I can feel her warmth. "Jade, look at me." At first she doesn't move, but finally she opens her eyes. She knows something is in here with her, but she still can't see me. I pull on our link, which is stronger now because I'm so close to her.

. . .

"Who's there?" she whispers out. "SiN?" Shaking her head, she closes her eyes. "Stop doing this to yourself, Jade. No one is coming for you, especially not him. Dreams are a waste of time, quit hoping for something that will never happen."

I know I'm wasting time watching her now that she has fallen back to sleep. I pull the locator thing they gave me off and drop it on the bed right next to her hand. The moment I let go of it. I expect it to disappear, but it doesn't. However, when I try to touch it again, my hand passes right through it.

I can't waste any more time here. I have to find a way in and try to see exactly what they are doing here, but this time when I get close to the door, it doesn't open. My first thought is to mist under it and I'm happily shocked when my body responds, as it always did.

Being able to travel like this makes maneuvering through the multiple tunnels much quicker as I don't have to hide or slide through the shadows. Zooming through this hallway as quickly as I can, I notice most are asleep. There are a few Jynrel guards, but they are just lounging around, most of them napping.

· · ·

THEY ARE ONLY WATCHING the females inside, but no one is guarding the doors, so they will be easily defeated. The level below this one is mainly machinery. The one above seems to be the offices and laboratories for the Chilton. So the females are all on the same level at least. Roughly, I have counted around twenty or so, but my female is the only human.

IMMEDIATELY, I push that thought out of my head. She is not mine and I am in no position in my life to make her, even though her words before seemed to tear my insides to pieces. I plan on helping them get her out of here and then it's every male for himself. Because I am not just going to sit around and wait for them to imprison me.

JUST AS I find an outer door, my mist fails me, and I practically fall to the floor. I instantly push myself up against the wall, waiting to see if anyone saw me. The door has an electronic pad on it and just as I start to reach for it. I find my eyes opening back on the Explorer.

Chapter Twenty-Two

Jade

THE LIGHTS COMING on wake me up, and my first thoughts are of SiN. He haunted my dreams last night, and once again, I could have sworn I saw him standing over my bed. It's amazing the things my mind will make up when it is desperate.

FEELING STIFF ALL OVER, I try to stretch out when my hand brushes against something. Picking up the small round disk, I wonder how it got here. It's not much larger than my palm, but there is a small yellow light blinking on it. Rubbing my fingers over it, I almost jerk out of my skin when a male's voice comes out of it.

"MISTRESS JADE, my name is SCOUT, and the device you hold in your palm is a locator beacon. I am monitoring your room and the adjoining hallway as we speak. The Chilten are making their morning rounds, but we have a few moments before they will arrive at your room.

"ONCE WE STOP TALKING, I need you to hide this device so that they are not advised of our arrival. I can't give you an exact time, but this rising you will be removed from this facility and returned to Darverius, where others of your kind are awaiting your return. The male you know as SiN has led us to you. We are in the process of rescuing you and the others being held at this facility. I hope my words give you some comfort. Try to hold on just a little longer. Don't fight them or do anything to injure yourself worse, we are coming for you."

TEARS FLOW DOWN MY CHEEKS, but I can't keep from smiling. "He is coming for me, never in my wildest dreams would I have allowed myself to believe that."

. . .

"Mistress Jade, the Chilten is almost at the door, but SiN asked me to tell you something. He said, '*The stars in the heavens would have to go out before he forgot you.*' Remember to hide the device."

Tucking the small disk underneath me, I had no longer straightened back up, when the door opens. Volten strolls in, looking at the pad in his hands. I try to calm myself, but the tears just won't stop.

"What has brought on this distress, Jade?"

"Just a bad dream."

"Our subconscious does get rather creative when we slumber. This rising we will start the retraction of your blood. I have convinced my superiors to allow me to take smaller amounts from you every rising instead of all at once. Hopefully, doing it this way will help you survive longer. They were not happy when I first approached them suggesting this, but after some rather heated conversations, they sided with me. I am going to mildly sedate you once again, as the needles are rather large and the location I need to pull the blood from can be painful. Please, try to lie as still as possible."

. . .

I ONLY HEAR pieces of what he says to me, as my heart is beating out of my chest. SiN coming is a fantasy I never would allow myself to dream of. I'm sure there is a side to this story I don't know or understand, but right now, I will allow my mind to believe he is coming simply for me.

THOSE BUBBLES APPEAR in my vision once again, and then there is a sharp pinch on the inside of my thigh and one on the inside of my arm. Blinking a few times, the room becomes fuzzy, and I am instantly nauseous, as it feels like I am being sucked dry.

"VOLTEN, I don't feel so good."

"FORGIVE ME, Jade, I believe it's draining too quickly. Let me make a few adjustments and let's get some liquids in you to help with the sugar loss."

A STRAW APPEARS NEXT to my mouth, and I greedily drink as much as I can before Volten pulls it away. "Thank you."

. . .

"You are most welcome, as soon as this session is over, you will have a few rotations to recover. I will be back shortly, there are others I need to tend. I can monitor your vitals from my Holo pad, but if you start to feel any worse, push that blue button on your bed."

If I couldn't still feel the small disk under me, I would be doubting I ever heard that voice earlier. Looking around, I can see the large vat that is now holding my blood. Every time it pulses, I can feel it pulling more of my blood out and the room starts to sway. I attempt to hit the button, but my arm won't respond.

My heart is beating so hard in my chest, I feel like I'm smothering. The pulls begin to be more aggressive, and I feel like I'm folding in on myself. Straining, I scream out, but it sounds like a squeak even to my own ears.

Collapsing back on the bed, I'm so weak I can't blink my eyes. I simply stare out at nothing. I should have known better than to fantasize or even wish that I was going to make it out of here. The darkness pulls at me, but I fight it. Because I know the moment I shut my eyes, it's all over. All my wants and dreams will be lost forever, but the shadows finally win, and I feel myself drifting away.

Chapter Twenty-Three

SiN

Father once again is sitting in the chair next to the bed. I don't recall getting in. I jump up and am only steps away from SCOUT when Father steps in front of me. How he got there quicker than I did, I have no idea.

"How the frack did I get here, Father?" I point at the male leaning casually against the wall. "That sorry prick did something to me didn't he?"

. . .

"I BROUGHT YOU HERE, SiN. It doesn't matter the who or why's. We need to stay on task here; did you find the female?"

THE SITUATION HAS me misting in and out for a few moments before I get a hold of my anger. "I'm tired of being your little experiment. This ends now, no more using me for your advantage or I promise you from this moment on my cooperation ends."

"SiN, you have my word it will never occur again. Not from anyone I have command of, anyway. Did you find anything helpful?"

PACING AROUND THE ROOM, I try to focus on what I saw. "Give me a second to sort through it. It's odd being there that way, it's like viewing things through a mirror. Things are not always as they appear or even where you think they are. I found an outer door we should be able to access. It appeared to be only used for maintenance. There was a shuttle bay, but it is too small for this ship. However, it might be possible to connect to that door I was telling you about with an atmospheric tunnel."

"WHAT ABOUT GUARDS?"

. . .

"I SAW A HANDFUL OF JYNREL, but nothing we can't deal with. I don't know if the Chilten will retaliate once we get inside, there are several of them on the premises. One thing I do know is we need to shut down their communications so that they can't call for backup. What are we going to do to the facility, destroy it?"

"WE SHOULD CONCENTRATE on the females for now and leave the place be. SCOUT will be installing micro-cameras and other equipment while we are inside so that we can get a better idea of what's going on here. If we can pull this off successfully, they will return in time. I think leaving the facility will give us some insights on what or who is doing these experiments out there. Once we have the proof we need, then we can and will take things to the next level."

"WHAT MAKES you think they won't shut it down after this?"

"SCOUT IS GOING to erase the main camera feeds. If we can corral all the Chilten in one area before we go inside, then they will have no way of knowing we were even there. He is going to plant false images of the females rioting, then escaping on their own."

. . .

"Master Sin, I managed to speak to Mistress Jade for a few moments. I needed her to hide that locator you placed on her bed and offered her a few words of comfort from you."

"What did you say to her?"

"That the stars in heaven would have to go out before you would forget her."

"I didn't say that."

"No, but you should have. Females need to know they are wanted or they give up the fight for survival and right now she needs all the encouragement she can get."

Suddenly I sway on my feet, and my heart starts beating irregularly. Father grabs my arm and then SCOUT is standing right in front of me. He puts one finger on my wrist, and I snarl down at him as Father holds me still.

. . .

"COMMANDER, Master SiN is experiencing the female's distress as his own. Her vital signs are dropping quickly. We need to leave now if we are going to save her in time. Master SiN, you need to push those feelings away and concentrate on steadying your own bodily functions at this time."

"YEAH, easier said than done. You just get me to that door, I'll be fine."

TORDAN APPEARS AT THE DOORWAY. "Come, I have our gear ready. The Explorer is lowering herself into position as we speak. Because of the storms coming off the Nebula, we have to time this just right."

NO ONE SAYS another word as we run towards a part of the ship I have not seen before. Tordan hands out portable breathers, and I hook mine on as I look out a small porthole in the ship's side, watching the dim lights of the facility get closer.

"YOU TWO STAY HERE, I can get in and out without anyone seeing me."

· · ·

Father shakes his head no. "I will be accompanying you."

"Look, it's not like I'm going to run off."

"Sin, I didn't say you were, but I will not remain on this ship while you put yourself in danger. Once the facility is secured, Tordan and SCOUT's job is to attach the tunnel and get the other females on board safely. SCOUT knows multiple languages and that will help them achieve this quickly. I will assist you with the Jynrel and any others who decide to interfere with the human female's removal. XuL and RaZ will stay on board as backup. Here put this in your ear so that you can communicate with everyone."

"I see you have worked it all out."

"It's kinda what I do."

"At least let me go ahead of you and see if anyone is around."

· · ·

"WE GO TOGETHER. You have no cause to concern yourself with me. I won't be seen unless I want to be."

WE APPROACH the outer doorway quickly. A small cable launches out of the ship, connecting us to the building, and then the atmospheric barrier of the Explorer opens up. Connecting to the line, I jump, hitting the door just slightly harder than I intended. The electronic door panel comes on the moment I touch it. SCOUT's voice sounds over the comm quietly. "SiN, give me a second to unlock the mechanism and pressurize the corridor."

THE DOOR POPS OPEN, and I mist inside. Turning back, I look for Father, only for him not to be there. He must have noticed my hesitation. "Proceed SiN, I'm right behind you."

"THE FRACK YOU ARE."

WHEN FATHER STEPS out of the shadows, I actually jerk back.

"YOU ARE NOT the only one who can shadow walk, Son. At least now you know who you got that talent from. Lead the way."

. . .

"SEE if you can keep up, old man."

A COUPLE of chuckles can be heard right after he growls. Misting through the hall, I head towards the first set of guards from behind. Making sure no one sees us, Father and I quickly overpower them. Then we gather the remaining guards on this floor up, securing them in one of the empty rooms. We are just shutting the door when I feel her distress.

MISTING down the hallway and into her room, I find myself standing over her, not believing my eyes. I was here just half a rotation ago, and she was fine. Now she is lying here, staring out at nothing. Her eyes are sunken in, and her skin is so pale she has turned gray. Shivers wrack her small frame as her whole body seems to be twitching. Instantly, I notice two huge needles sticking out of her delicate skin. Just as I reach for one, Father grabs my arm.

"DON'T; she might bleed out before we can stop what they have started. We need to get this machine turned off first."

. . .

INSTEAD OF DOING as I am told, I just stand here watching her fade right in front of me.

"SIN, snap out of it and help me."

WITHOUT THINKING, I start yanking plugs and wires out of the walls until all the machines stop. Putting my head on her chest, I can barely hear her heart beating. Her breathing is so light that her chest isn't even moving.

FATHER IS TALKING to someone in the background, but I can't seem to hear him. *I did this to her. It's my fault that she is here in the first place. If I hadn't done the things I did and if I hadn't forced her to come with me to my shuttle. She would never have been taken. I truly am a monster!*

FATHER REACHES DOWN, touching the side of her neck and I have to make myself not attack him.

"YES, I can still feel a heartbeat, but it's faint, ANDI!"

. . .

THE NEXT THING I KNOW, a miniature male is hovering above her stomach wearing a weird hat and matching suit.

"COMMANDER, I came as soon as SCOUT messaged me."

"THANK YOU, ANDI, we need your advice on how to proceed. I was unable to connect with Father because of the solar storm the Nebula is producing. The Explorer has a healing chamber, but I fear she is past the point it would do her any good. Also, the Explorer's system doesn't have the knowledge of the human anatomy that you do. What can be done to save this female?"

THE LITTLE HOLOGRAM male goes quiet for a second. "From what I can tell, they have withdrawn too much of her blood. According to their medical charts, she was already malnourished and weak upon arrival, and they did nothing to reverse that before hooking her up to this machine. They had very little concern for her wellbeing.

"HER HEART IS STRUGGLING and is at the point of failure as we speak, and she seems to have already slipped into a mild unconsciousness. Her survival rate in this current condition is nine percent. Even if you could start an IV and transfusion successfully without her veins blowing, she wouldn't make it more than a few more hours."

HE HOVERS CLOSER to her face. "Would one of you move her head to the side, please?" I gently turn her head over.

"WHO BIT HER?"

"I DID, I didn't know it would … I didn't know what I was doing, and still don't, but it has made this link between us. That's how I found her."

"Do you love or care about this girl?"

"I DON'T EVEN KNOW HER." I snarl back defensively.

THE HOLOGRAM PACES BACK and forth. "That's a shame. I can tell by the marks on her skin that her life up until now has not been kind. Commander, my recommendation is to let her go, not all can be saved. Life has not been good to this poor girl, and sometimes the most generous thing we can do is let them return to their gods. I will try to do a facial recognition and run it through my archives of Earth. Maybe I can at least find out who she was and how she got here."

"All I know is her name is Jade. Mystic could probably tell you more."

Father looks over at me and then back down to the hologram, a sad expression on his face. For some reason, the fact that everyone has given up enrages me.

"What, that's it? She is still breathing, right this moment she is still alive. That means there is still hope. What do you expect me to do simply stand here and watch her fade away? She is the whole reason I'm standing here healed and alive. No, I won't accept your answer. Father, help me get this crap off and out of her. You said there was a healing chamber on the ship. We will take her there. I am not just going to let her die."

Gently, I start drawing the long needle out of her arm. I expect her to bleed heavily once I remove them, but only a few drops form around the holes. Just as I lift her up into my arms, I hear her chest rattle. There is no missing the sound of death coming for her.

.   .   .

"Come on, Jade, hold on just a little longer."

"Son, put her down, let her go in peace."

Pulling her closer to me, I will my strength into her as I feel our bond fading away. My heart starts beating wildly in my chest as I look over at him, feeling more helpless than I have ever felt in my life. Anyone who was ever important to me is gone, now I get to watch her go too.

She gasps against my chest, and I look down quickly. She whispers something that I can't make out before her eyes roll back in her head.

"Noooooo!" I scream out. "Jade, come on, talk to me Angel, give me some hope here. Don't you give up Jade, fight, dammit.

"Did either of you hear her?" I feel like I'm on the verge of a complete meltdown. Why her words are suddenly so important to me I don't know, but for the first time in my life. I send a prayer out for someone other than my selfish self. *"Please, Lord of Light show me how to correct the wrong I have done to her."*

"So, you do care," the holo male says. "Master SiN, lay her down quickly, don't argue with me, just do it. If you want to save her life, you have to do exactly as I say." I don't even hesitate to do as the little hologram male says.

"You must drain the rest of her blood from her body."

"What?"

"You have to bite her as you did before. Then the very moment before her heart stops completely, she has to ingest your blood. You will probably have to force her mouth open, but she must swallow as much of your blood as possible. There is no time for questions, just do it!"

My fangs lengthen instinctively. Biting her gently, it takes a few pulls for her nectar to reach my lips. But nothing before, or up till date, has ever tasted this divine to me. Lost in the taste of her blood, I almost miss the sound of her struggling heart.

UNLATCHING MY FANGS, I use one of my claws to cut the skin open on my wrist. When I tilt her head back, her mouth falls open on its own. I watch my blood drip into her mouth, but she doesn't swallow any of it. Father reaches over and starts massaging her neck and I finally see it start slipping down her throat. Two heartbeats later, her heart stops and I roar out in defeat as her body starts to turn cold in my hands.

I TURN my fury towards the holographic male. "You said this would work! I will find out where you originate from and tear you to pieces. Do you hear me? All we did was quicken her death, taking any and all chances of her survival away."

"CALM DOWN, Master SiN. Things are not as they seem."

"THE FRACK THEY'RE NOT, she is dead!"

"MASTER SIN, we don't know that for sure at this time. The process is not instantaneous. The next few risings will tell if you were able to change her in time. Take Jade back to the

Explorer and clean her up, make her as comfortable as possible. Watch her body for any signs of change, if this is successful, they will be significant. If her body doesn't reject your blood, you will know in three risings one way or another."

"Ok, you all must think I'm simple or something, but I am the one holding her here. She has no heartbeat, she isn't breathing, but according to you somehow, she is just going to wake up in a couple risings like nothing is wrong. Rise from the dead like nothing happened?"

"Master SiN, there are some things that cannot be truly explained. Don't lose your faith yet, but be prepared for the repercussions of your actions, as you have just bound this female to you for eternity. By the way, she said, '*You came*' I am going to assume you understand the meaning behind that statement."

"I told her I was coming, but I don't think she ever believed me. I never gave her a reason to. All she has received from me is snarls and disbelief. She deserves better than me."

"Then my first piece of advice, Master SiN, is to become the male she deserves My name is ANDI, and I will be available for any consultation you may need, all you need to do is call out."

FATHER TURNS away when he hears voices in the hallway. "Tordan is leading the other females to the ship. It seems they were able to sedate all the Chilten at once in one of the laboratories. When they are on board, SiN, I will return for you and your female."

I NOD and gather her back up into my arms. Brushing her hair off her face, I pull her in close, rocking her back and forth. *What have I done?* Is the one thing rolling through my mind constantly. If by some miracle she does survive this, she will despise me for taking away all her choices. *How do I make this right? I don't want to feel this way about another person. So why do I believe she is going to make me eat those words?*

Chapter Twenty-Four

SiN

I BROUGHT her back to the ship. Then washed every inch of her by hand because I was scared the ionizer would damage her skin worse. Finding a soft gown in one of the drawers. I drape it over her small frame. Then I sit down in the chair next to the bed, watching her every move.

IT'S BEEN two risings and besides her body no longer feeling cold to the touch, there hasn't been a single change. Father and Tordan have both stopped in multiple times, but I am in no mood for conversation. We should have returned to Darverius within the next rising, but Tordan and XuL decided to return as many of the females as they could to their prior homes if they were close.

My mind is all over the place. From praying she gets better, to what do I have to offer her if she does? To will I be arrested the moment this ship lands? Rubbing a weary hand over my face, I start to close my eyes for a second when I swear. I see her hand move.

Instantly I am at her side, taking her fragile hand in my own. Rubbing my hand down each finger admiring how anything this small could be this strong. Bathing her really put things in perspective for me. I can't imagine what type of monster would inflict such pain on anything this delicate. It's almost like whoever scarred her never marked her in the same place twice. They deliberately were marring every inch of her skin. What type of anger or jealousy would make someone do this? Lord of Light knows if it's the last thing I ever do. I will destroy them if I ever find out a name. I might be labeled a monster, but I can't imagine doing what was done to her ... to another.

The door opens and RaZ comes strolling in. He doesn't say a word at first, just looks at us both on the bed.

. . .

"WHAT DO YOU WANT, WING BOY?"

"THOUGHT I MIGHT BE of service, Mist boy. You need to go get a bag of yuck and clean up. She will need you at your strongest when she wakes up."

"IF SHE WAKES UP."

"SHE WILL, I can already tell. The changes are small right now, but if you know what to look for, you can see them. She will be terrified when she awakens, and stronger than you may be able to handle alone."

"WHAT ARE YOU TALKING ABOUT? She is just a tiny little thing."

"THE DELICATE LITTLE female that needed you for protection will no longer be the same. She will be a weapon no one anticipates. You didn't go through any other changes than your diet because your body already had some very unique upgrades. That won't be the case with her. Everything will be a new experience, including being around others. Smell, sight, strength, all of that will become overwhelming the moment she opens her eyes. You will have to teach her how to adapt and be around others."

"I DON'T KNOW if you got the memo, Wing boy, but I am not going to be around to do that. The moment this ship lands, I have two choices. Run like hell, as I have heard the females say, or stay, and be imprisoned for life. Neither of those options have a female attached to them anywhere."

"THOSE ARE things to worry about at another rising. I will sit with her go on and take a moment to yourself. When you come back, you will see things more clearly. You stink go get cleaned up."

RELUCTANTLY, I leave the room. Taking a couple of the bags out of the warmer, I gag at the taste as I force myself to swallow this nasty stuff. When I get out of the Ionizer, I admit that it feels nice to be clean. Redressing with a thought, I hurry back to Jade. When I come through the doorway, I am shocked at what I'm seeing.

RAZ IS STILL STANDING in the same spot with a smirk on his face … I point at her. "I didn't do anything, but sometimes we can't see the forest for the trees. My Katherine loves that saying."

JADE IS PRACTICALLY GLOWING, even though she lay deathly still. Sitting down next to her, I run my hand down her cheek, noticing immediately that the scar that had run along the edge is fading. Jerking my hand back, I look up at RaZ. "What is happening to her?"

"SHE IS a human being turned into a vampire. Vampire is a term that the humans gave the ones who drink blood to survive. To make a long story short, when Grandfather and the other Elders crashed onto Earth, they were starving because they ran out of the Blood Beet fruit that our kind depends on to survive. One of the Elders went looking for substance and without going into all the details, he figured out they could survive on human blood. From my understanding, they all turned into monsters, draining everyone and anything they could get their hands on. Because the taste and the feedings were like being high on drugs.

"GRANDFATHER WAS the first to see what they were doing and what they had become. He apparently separated himself from the others, but not before he realized they had spread an unknown virus from their bite to some of the survivors that had been bitten. In other words, they created these Vampires, a race of new humans remade by the aliens that had crashed on their planet.

"AFTER SOME TIME, the ones that were changed had to go into hiding as they were being hunted because of the lives they took. On Earth, she wouldn't be able to go out into the sunlight, and certain minerals would be poisonous to her. So you will have to watch her and make sure that she doesn't start to burn on Darverius. There is no way of knowing how our sun's will affect her. The pain would be excruciating and sometimes deadly if she is exposed for too long.

"WHEN YOU BIT HER, you injected her with a virus that is changing what they call her DNA. This change affects her not only internally, but externally. When she awakes, and she will awaken, she will no longer be the girl you knew before, on the inside or out. She will be frozen in time, never to age again, just like my Katherine and Victoria.

"IF SHE BECOMES INJURED, she will heal at such a rapid rate you will think it's instantaneous, but she will still feel pain and heartache the same as you do. She is linked to your life force, so as long as you live, she will as well. Her body is healing from the inside out, but it's also remaking her into her best version.

"The Healing chamber did something similar to Kira. When she woke up, she said she felt like they put her into someone else's body. I have heard her tell Victoria many times that she doesn't recognize the woman staring back at her in the mirror because even on earth, she never looked like that. The vampire gene creates a seduction, a smell that can be used to lure others to them, it makes them irresistible to the ones they want to feed from. In other words, every male will want her. So if you don't give her what she needs another sure will.

"I can already see her skin changing and her hair becoming thicker, more luxurious. She will be a rare beauty on the outside, but the same fragile female in her mind, if she can't handle the changes forced upon her. I asked, but ANDI is not for sure if she will regain her memories. I hope for her sake she doesn't, because this will be hard enough without you there to help her through it.

"She will need to feed and right now you will be her favorite flavor, but you will have to watch her strength. She won't understand that she can crush skulls with her hands for a while and she can do some real damage to you if you're not careful. On Earth, Tyberius, our grandfather, and the other elders had strict rules about changing humans. Because some went mad with a feeding lust that they couldn't control.

"HER MIND HAS ALREADY BEEN TAMPERED with and this may push her past a point where she is more animal than human. Now all of this is the worst-case scenario, but I thought you should know the possible outcomes. Expect the worst and hope for the best, Mist boy. I would say at the rate she is changing now, she will awaken in half a rotation. Father is putting off landing, trying to give you some time with her.

"WHILE YOU HAVE BEEN HOLED up in here. He has been on one call after another, talking to the Elders about you. He fights for your freedom even though you don't deserve it. The only reason I'm tolerating you is because you not only hold your life in your hands, but this female's, and now Father, who blames himself for the things you have done."

"I DIDN'T ASK for his help or your advice, Wing boy."

.   .   .

RaZ's wings rattle in annoyance. "How many more are you going hurt before you finally get it? Or are you simply too stubborn to realize there is more to this world than yourself?"

Before he can say a word, he turns and walks out the door. I noticed earlier that they no longer had the clear shield up that traps me in this room, but I no longer have the urge to flee. RaZ's words echo through my head only confusing me more.

I am sitting here watching Jade, caught up in my own thoughts, when Father's voice sounds next to me. Jerking, he puts a large hand on my shoulder. "I didn't mean to startle you, but I have some news that I thought you would like to know. ANDI please proceed where you left off."

The small hologram male pops up next to me on the bed. He hovers casually above Jade. "Oh, she is going to be a looker. Look at those cheekbones and all that pretty hair." He whistles an odd sound, and I hear Father chuckle behind me.

"Forgive me, but she took my breath away."

. . .

SNARLING, I say, "You don't need to breathe."

"HA, very true Master SiN, but if…" He fans his face like he is hot, and I am truly confused. "I am relieved to see the change is progressing as it should. I have some information about our little Jade here. The things I found are shocking. We know her name is Becca Jade Simpson. She was twenty-eight when she was taken walking home from a late night shift at the hospital where she was employed. She had no living family or close friends, and that may have been how she was targeted.

"APPARENTLY, no one recorded her missing at first. Then it was only done because she had not reported to work for several days. In the paper, one of her co-workers mentioned that she prided herself on her punctuality and when she didn't show up, they knew something was wrong. The part that really shocked me was when she was taken. The limited records I have of her are because she went missing before their social media stage. She was grabbed in the early 1970s, that's about fifty years before our Kira. That means the Korgon were taking females from Earth long before we realized. That also means that there could be a lot more out there than we originally thought.

. . .

"Now that the Commander has made it known that the species is now under his protection, things may get bad for them. Commander, you may want to make an amendment to that order. Telling anyone who is harboring a human, that they can drop them off here without any charges being pressed or questions asked. Hopefully, this will keep them from being treated the way our poor Jade here was. If I find out anything else, I will contact you immediately. I must return to the Traveler; she is a female that demands my constant attention."

Father also starts to leave only to turn back right before he gets to the door. "I thought you would like to know as much about her as possible before she awakens. We still can't pinpoint who owned her or how long she was awake before she came to be in the forest, but I will continue to work on that. She has been in our world for quite some time, and they have hidden her right under our noses. Remember, SiN, I am here if you need me."

"Thank you, Father."

He nods, and I can tell my words shock him. The bad part is, they did me too, the moment they left my lips.

Chapter Twenty-Five

Jade

SITTING STRAIGHT UP in the bed, I gasp out in terror. My eyes dart around, looking for anything familiar only to find everything is unfamiliar. Someone touching my shoulder has me striking out, knocking whomever it is away from me. Before I can blink, I find myself standing on the bed, a hiss leaving my throat as I peer at the male laying on the floor in front of me.

MY EYES DEVOUR HIS BEAUTY, but it's the beating of his heart that is drowning out everything else. He holds his hand out, saying something to me, but I can't hear anything besides the sound of his blood rushing through his veins. Something primal clicks inside of me and I snarl out, "MINE!"

Before I realize what I have done, I have him pinned down underneath me, my legs straddling his hips securely, making the gown I have on, ride up. Holding him tightly, my fangs sink deeply into his tender flesh. The taste of his blood, the essence that provides him life has me moaning out in pleasure as I grind myself against him. His muscles tense under me, but he doesn't fight against my hold and I'm almost disappointed in how easily he has given in.

Opening my eyes, I can see the intricate details of his skin, each crease, every line. I am amazed at the texture of his black hair, as a few pieces have fallen against my cheek that I have pressed against his.

My hands roam freely over his masculine figure. No rational thoughts seem to surface because my need for him is so great. Taking a hard pull from his neck, I savor the taste of not only his blood, but his skin against my tongue. I can't seem to get close enough as I rub my entire body on his, wishing I could pull him inside me somehow. That's when I realize I can.

. . .

WRENCHING AWAY, I lick and nip at his neck, making my way down his chest slowly. The claws on my fingertips scratch him, leaving small trails of blood that I lap up eagerly as I make my way down to my final goal. When I come to his pants, I growl and hiss because they are blocking my way further.

WITHOUT ASKING, I rip the entire front of his pants off, grabbing his long hard shaft in my hand, caressing his balls gently. I feel him tense up when I start to lower my head. It makes me angry when a strong grip fastens in my hair, stopping me from going any further. Looking up at him as I work him up and down aggressively. The veins pulsing in his shaft call to me as a small white bead pearls at the top of its large dark gray mushroom head. "Mine," I snarl up at him as he smiles down at me.

"IT'S YOURS, but no biting unless you want me to bite back."

PONDERING ON THAT FOR A MOMENT, a mischievous thought comes to me. Licking him from his balls all the way up his shaft. I make sure my fangs catch his delicate skin just enough to cut him slightly. Then I lap up the small amount of blood until he is practically panting as he squirms in pleasure and pain beneath me.

.   .   .

He still has his hand wrapped up in my hair and I know he is talking to me, but right now the only sound I can hear is his heart shoving his blood through his veins. Refusing to deny myself any longer. I let go of my prize for a second and climb back up onto his stomach. Looking down at the bright yellow eyes and the wicked smile of the man underneath me.

"Frack Jade, in all my rotations I would have never dreamed you would wake up like this. Sweet thing, you need to calm down a little. Now don't get me wrong even though I was shocked at first. I am willing and able I just don't want you to regret this later. Do you know me?"

"You're MINE."

"Yes, apparently I am, at least for the moment. That is, until you decide you can do better, but do you remember my name?"

His shaft is hard, pulsing beneath me eagerly. I can feel myself getting wetter as I rub my folds up and down his length. Throwing my head back, I growl as I grab it in my hand. Positioning him at my entrance, I impaled myself. He yells out, clutching me by my waist as I grind down hard. His girth fills me so completely I have to take a moment to adjust to his size.

ROLLING MY HIPS, I slowly start lifting myself up and down. One of his hands cup my breast rolling my nipple between his thumbs while the other grips my hip tightly. My hands skim over his chest lightly before I come absorbed with the fullness of him inside me. Each thrust of his hips brings us both closer to something that feels just out of grasp.

HE REACHES IN BETWEEN US, pinching and rolling my pleasure nub quickly, and I shatter into a million pieces. Falling towards him, I latch onto his neck once more as he thrusts inside of me. The moment my fangs slide into his skin he roars out as his own release pulses within me. Clutching me tightly to him, my mind starts to settle.

THE PRESENCE of another coming into our space has me jerking up, and I hiss out. "Leave, imposter." At the stranger, who looks the same as the one that's MINE.

· · ·

Laughter rumbles underneath me as he holds me firmly so that I can't escape. "Father, you may want to shut the door, she is a little possessive right now."

"Sorry, I heard you yell … Ughh yeah, leaving now. Lord of Light, I think I am going to be scarred for life."

The door closes, and I lay back down draped over his chest. His heart beat and familiar smell calms my thoughts. Giving me a moment to realize he is rubbing my back gently, saying a name over and over. Wait a minute, that's my name, *I am Jade*. The second I realize what I'm doing, I jerk back, horrified when I see what I have done to him. His neck looks like something rabid chewed on him and his body is scratched all over. I can't believe he let me do that to him.

Crawling away, his seed drips down my thighs and suddenly I am terrified of the repercussions of my actions. *What have I done?* I have to get out of here. Looking for a way to escape, a hand shoots out, but I dart around it towards the door. Just as I step through, another catches me. This one smells wrong and I fight against his hold, scratching and clawing, trying to free myself from his massive arms.

• • •

MY MIND IS SO FILLED with terror that I don't realize he isn't fighting me back. Everything is too bright and loud. Holding my hands over my ears, I try to drown out the sound of all the heart beats around me. *Who are these males, how did I get here?*

THE MALE HOLDING me takes a couple steps back inside the room. The blood on his arms and the scratches on his cheeks make me look away. As he hands me back to the one I just ran from, I whisper, "I am sorry, please don't hurt me." I know better than to fight back. I need to hide, get out of sight so that they can't find me.

WHEN A LARGE SET of hands pulls me close, I flinch. When his familiar smell surrounds me, I turn, immediately tucking myself into his colossal frame.

SHUTTING MY EYES. I try to make myself focus on what is going on around me. The floor under my feet has a slight vibration, so we must be on a ship. I can hear the air circulating through the vents and other people's voices, but they're not close. The male who is holding me smells right, and I feel safe in his arms, but I know that's all a lie. There is no safe place. What is happening to me? Was that another dream? Did I really bite and feed from … what's his name again …

SiN? Yes, that's who this is, ohhh no … he is a bad guy, or is he? I don't know, but suddenly I'm scared.

WORDS, there are too many words, everything is too loud. I try to push the images of the things that have happened to me out of my mind, but the pain is overwhelming. Everyone keeps hurting me, but why? Who are these people, these things? A tree … I found comfort within a tree. I must find my way back there. I have to find a way to quiet all the thoughts, all this noise. She … Mystic was the only safe place I can remember. Without further thought, I immediately start fighting against the hold SiN has on me.

"JADE, stop before you hurt yourself. Can you hear me?"

HIS VOICE MAKES the noise stop and I try to focus on it instead of the rage and uncertainty flooding my system. I look up, as he peers down at me, *is he talking to me? Yes … I think I am this Jade.* I nod yes.

"THERE YOU ARE. Do you know who I am?"

"YOU ARE SiN," I say without further thought.

. . .

"TAKE A DEEP BREATH, Jade. You are safe, no one is going to hurt you. I am going to let go and I want you to stay still so we can talk. Can you understand me? You need to take a couple deep breaths, your emotions, and actions, are all over the place."

I NOD MY HEAD AGAIN, but this time I feel something wet on my chin. I reach up, wiping my hand across it, only to find it covered in blood. The sight of it suddenly has me trembling all over. A small cry leaves my lips, as I can't seem to figure out what's real and what's not.

HE GRABS MY HAND. "Hey, look at me. You have done nothing wrong, no one is going to hurt you, come on, let's go get you cleaned up, ok?" He must have taken my silence as an acceptance. "Jade, you have been asleep for a long time. There are some changes that we need to talk about, but you're going to be fine now. I promise I won't let anyone hurt you."

REACHING UP, I trace the marks I made on his neck. My eyes get bigger as I watch the bruising lighten unnaturally quick. "SiN, I did bad things to you. I thought it was a dream again and I'm so sorry. I know what it's like to be forced to do something you don't want to. Please, don't hurt me."

"WHAT HAPPENED to the tigress that woke up a little bit ago? Where did this scaredy cat come from? Sweet thing, I am twice your size, you didn't force me to do anything I didn't want to do. The moment you opened those beautiful violet eyes of yours, I was a goner. You had me worried these last couple of rotations. You need not concern your pretty little head about what just happened. To be honest, I think I just lived out one of my biggest fantasies. We can play that game as much as you want, anytime you want. I liked how aggressive you were."

TAKING ME BY THE HAND, he gently pulls me into another room. Standing behind me at the sink, he washes my hands, taking the time to clean each finger so there isn't a speck left on them. His large body curved around mine seems to have my entire focus until I look up.

A WHIMPER LEAVES my lips at the sight standing before me. His eyes meet mine in the mirror as he reaches up, wiping a small red spot off my cheek. A cheek that is no longer scarred. My large violet eyes stare back at the stranger wearing my face, or what I think is my face.

. . .

REACHING UP SLOWLY, I watch my hand move in the mirror like it's someone else's and trace the place where the scar used to be. That's when I notice the skin on my hands is smooth, and my arms are no longer dotted with burn marks or … sliced to pieces from the whip. A whip, I can remember plainly now, but that seems to be about it. I still have no idea where I came from before being dumped in the forest.

I PUSH BACK AGAINST HIM, but he grabs my upper arms, holding me in place. "What, how, who is this?"

"FORGIVE ME JADE, but you were dying and I … well I just couldn't let that happen. I promise, I will try to explain what I can before we land, but we don't have much time. You have changed on the outside, but you are still you. Does that make any sense at all? Lord, I suck at this."

I SHAKE MY HEAD NO. "The scars … are they all gone?"

"FROM THE OUTSIDE, yes. The ones in your mind, no."

. . .

"WHAT ARE you going to do with me now? Why did you save me? I prayed that you would come, then I prayed you wouldn't."

"I DON'T REALLY HAVE a good answer to either of those questions. While I would love to claim that it's because you saved my life, I would only be deceiving both of us. You are experiencing the pull to me the same as I am towards you. I'm yours no different than you are mine. It's a lot to take in all at once, so try not to focus on any one thing. Give yourself and the thought of us some time."

"SIN, can I have a minute to myself? Everything is so loud, and I feel strange all over. My mind is torn and you being this close … it is taking all of my control not to attack you again. Why do I feel this way? I bit you, for God's sake, SiN."

"WE CAN REPLAY that little moment back there in that room any time you want, Angel. I already told you that. It wasn't like you held me down and took advantage of me. The way you woke up was natural. You would not have acted that way if your mate had not been in the room, but I was.

· · ·

"YOUR BODY simply took what it needed. The fact that you fed and met the needs consuming you simply calmed your mind enough that you could think clearly. Now that I see how tormented you are by your actions, maybe I should have kept you hungry.

"DON'T LOOK at me like that, I am just teasing you. I'll be in the other room, take your time. There's supposed to be some clothes in here for you as well. Yell out if you need me."

I WATCH him walk away as I gaze through the mirror. My mind flashes back to the first time I laid eyes on him, and what bad shape he was in. Even injured I was drawn to him, but now he is so beautiful he is hard to look upon. His voice is pleasing to me like velvet soft and smooth in a world that is so full of noise. Now, his touch is gentle, not rough as it was in the past. The way I felt in his arms earlier is too confusing to think about, so I push it away.

MY GUMS FEEL ODD, and I open my mouth, only to find a set of fangs. Jerking back away from the mirror, I can now see my body fully. I yank off the thin covering I've had on this whole time and stare at a complete stranger looking back at me. Running my eyes over this new body of mine, there is no missing the high breasts, long tapered muscular legs, thin waistline, or the flat stomach. My dark hair falls in long, thick waves past my butt. I am looking at a young woman in her prime. What type of sorcery can remake a tortured body into this? Or maybe the question is, *who's new body … am I wearing?*

I ALMOST JUMP out of my new skin when a small face appears in the mirror. "Hello Jade, my name is SAGE, and I am pleased to see you up and about. I'm sure you have a million questions about what has happened to you and what's going on. Hopefully, by the time you leave this room, I will have answered most of them. We don't have a lot of time, as the Explorer will be docking with Falcor within the next hour. So, let's get you into the Ionizer and into something more comfortable. While you're there, I will try my best to fill you in on the events that have led up to this rotation.

"MISTRESS KATHERINE and Victoria will be awaiting you on Solanar when the shuttle lands. I promise anything I leave out, they will be able to answer."

CLOSING MY EYES, I rub my head, talking to myself. *'There are no talking faces in the mirror. None of this is real, you have snapped and are simply making up things as you go Jade.'* That is, until she giggles, and something touches me on the arm.

. . .

WHEN I OPEN my eyes back up, she is now floating midair right in front of me. Tilting her head a little, she looks me over. "Oh, your eyes are stunning. I must try them for myself, I have never seen that color before."

THE NEXT THING I KNOW, my own eyes are staring back at me.

"WHAT DO YOU THINK?" She twirls around, the skirt she is wearing flaring out playfully around her small see-through legs. I can't help but smile at her enthusiasm.

"YOU ARE QUITE BEAUTIFUL. What is your name again?"

"I AM SAGE and I promise we will be great friends. As you can see, I have taken the best of all of my friends and incorporated them ... well into me."

"YOU KNOW MORE LIKE ME? HUMANS?"

"OH, yeah, like I said, we have a lot to talk about, but first things first. I have learned quickly that getting clean and being in comfy clothes opens the mind, especially for us girls.

Coffee apparently is also a miracle cure, would you like some?"

I SNARL my nose at the thought. "No, but thanks."

"OK, THEN COME ON, FOLLOW ME."

I WALK behind the floating girl as she rattles on about how nice the refreshing rooms are in the Explorer. Following her instructions, I step up onto a circular device and a mist settles around me for a second before warm air dries me off just as quickly. Oddly enough, when she motions for me to follow her. I feel clean all over and my hair is even dry.

SEVERAL DRAWERS SLIDE OUT, and she motions for me. "Take whatever you need, there are panties in different sizes and styles available. Once you're done, we will go into the closet and find something suitable. After you are dressed, we will talk while I fix your hair. Just don't freak out on me while I change."

THE NEXT THING I know she is standing solid right next to me. A hiss leaves my throat before I can stop it.

. . .

"I TOLD you not to freak out."

"BUT HOW DID YOU … I mean you were in the mirror and then floating, and now you are standing next to me."

"YEAH, my story would open up a whole other bucket of worms, and we sure don't have time to sort through that right now, but you will get used to me just popping up. Hurry up chick, throw some clothes on. I decided while you were in the Ionizer to see if ANDI had time to pop in to fill you in on a few things. He has quite a bit more knowledge on you and the others than I do. So we will be learning a few things together."

GRABBING the first thing I see, I jerk a sundress over my head. The moment I am dressed, she yells out.

"ANDI, YOU CAN COME IN NOW."

ANOTHER FLOATING THING APPEARS, obviously male, as he is dressed in a gray suit with a matching top hat and cane. "Mistress Jade, it's good to see you up and about and looking so lovely. Since we don't have much time, we need to get right to it. Have you ever heard of a Vampire?"

"YOU MEAN DRACULA? Well, I believe so, but those were just made-up stories."

HE POINTS AT MY MOUTH. "Are you so sure about that Mistress Jade?"

I SIT down in a chair in front of SAGE while she plays with my hair, listening to ANDI tell me about the things that had happened to me. SiN sticks his head in the room when he hears me talking to the others and instead of leaving, he settles on the bed listening. At first, I am convinced they are just making this crap up, but all the evidence I really needed was staring back in the mirror.

"So, what you two are saying is that I am now Earth's version of a Vampire. I may not be able to tolerate sunlight, but I am stronger and faster than most. Now, my life span is linked to SiN's, who because of the charges against him, may not be around much longer. The reason why I attacked him earlier is because my alien vampire genes recognized him as my soul mate and this gene demanded that I mark him. So afterwards, because I had no control, SiN looked like a rabid animal had attacked him. Well, I am sure that's got to be a turn on for most men. Whatever.

"Now make sure I have this right. If I feed from anyone other than him, they will taste bad to me, most will even smell bad. I can survive on bagged blood even though it's nasty. Do I have all the basics, right?"

The little holo guy smirks before shaking his head yes.

"SiN, what are your thoughts on all of this? Did you know any of this before you changed me? Did you know you were going to have a stalker for the rest of your existence? Who would want to chew and suck on you every time she got the munchies?"

Everyone but me laughed at that last part.

"I knew pieces of all this, Jade, but I didn't have a lot of time to consider how you would feel about it though. You have to know I am just as drawn to you as you are to me. Yes, I agree the circumstances are not what either of us wanted, but maybe it's what we both needed. My choices up to date apparently have not been the best. As stubborn as I have been, I would have fought this attraction I have towards you until I destroyed us both. I refused to depend on or need another, and I would have been wrong. It bothers me how tightly you are bound to me. I have done a lot of things I'm not proud of, but you don't deserve to be punished for my bad decisions.

"As far as I know I will be arrested as soon as this ship lands. I have nothing to offer you but pain and heartache. If we had met in another lifetime … well there is not since wishing for things to be other than they are, but I want you to know I do wish things were different. I will speak to father, even though he owes me nothing. Hopefully, he will find a way for your life to be spared when they take mine."

"What, you're just giving up?"

"You don't understand."

"Well, then make me."

. . .

"Look, Jade, I can't change who I am, where I come from, or my circumstances any differently than you can. You got caught in my web of destruction and believe me I am sorry about that. If I were a better male, I would say go find you someone who would treat you the way you deserve, but the very thought of another holding or feeding you tears me to pieces on the inside. I know I have no right to feel that way and that you deserve your happiness, too. I just wish it was with me. You want to know the last thing that went through my mind when I woke up and found you standing over me?"

"What?"

"I thought you were a violet-eyed Angel. In my wildest dreams, I couldn't have ever imagined anything like you. You stood there so bravely, even with my hand grasp around your throat and all I could see was my future in your eyes. You would have done better to have let me die in that tree."

"Is that how you feel about me, because I can say the same thing, SiN?"

"No, Jade, your light was not ready to be vanquished."

. . .

"If I am to believe the words you have just spoken then I am the light to your darkness. Then let's figure this out together, no God would be cruel enough to take you from me the moment I realize you could be mine."

Before I can respond a voice comes across the room. "Master SiN, the Commander is expecting you in the shuttle bay. We have docked with Falcor, and your escort is awaiting."

I watch as he pulls himself off the bed. He runs a hand through his long black hair and with a sad look my way he starts to walk past me. Jumping up, I grab his arm, stopping him. SiN strokes the back of his hand down my cheek. "I am glad that mark is gone, but you were just as beautiful to me then as you are now. Forgive me, Jade." He pulls me near, kisses my forehead, then walks away.

I stand here for a second stunned. *No,* I refuse to remain here and let life tear us apart. Running out of the room, I head towards the voices in the hallway, screaming his name. I round a corner only to find myself caught up in his arms as he had turned back when he heard me calling out for him.

· · ·

WRAPPING my legs around his waist, I hug him close. Red tears flow down my cheeks as I tuck my head into his neck. "Please, I can't lose you." I feel a slight tremble pulse through his body and the next thing I know he is unwinding me from him and handing me to another.

"WING BOY, I'm handing you the only thing I care about in this world. Please take care of her."

"YOU HAVE MY WORD, Mist boy. She will come to no harm."

Chapter Twenty-Six

SiN

I HAVE DONE a lot of things in my lifetime that were difficult, but walking away from Jade while she fought to get to me is ripping me apart. I know the words RaZ spoke to me were true, as I could clearly see how this was also bothering him as he struggled to keep hold of her.

WIPING a stray tear off my face, I head towards Father, who has been watching all of this from the entrance to the shuttle bay. All I want to do is run back, grab her in my arms, and flee; it's taking everything in me to stay on this course.

· · ·

WHEN I START to pass Father, he grabs my arm, stopping me. "SiN, I know what you are thinking right now, and I caution you to not act rashly. I need you to trust me, Son. I know I have not earned that right, nor have I proved myself worthy of it in your eyes. However, this is one moment in time, I need you to set aside our differences and listen to me. Our existence is made up of hills and valleys, Son, but if you look hard enough. You will still see the wonders that have been granted to you. Even the smallest blessings are still blessings to cherish."

"ALL I ASK OF YOU, Father, is that you make sure no matter the outcome, that she will be protected and cared for?"

"YOU HAVE MY WORD. She not only has my protection, but that of all your brothers."

I CAN STILL HEAR her crying behind me, and I know if I don't get off this ship, no amount of promises will keep me on this track. "Well then, Father, we better get on with it before my heart shatters and my instincts take over."

I NO MORE THAN step past him when a regiment of guards wearing the colors of the Elder court approach me. "SiN, last living heir to the family of Yamamura, son of Commander DaR, and grandson of Elder Tyberius. We are here at the decree of the Elder Courts to take you into custody to be tried next rising for the criminal charges that have been obtained against you. Commander DaR has given his word that you will come with us peacefully, so we will not publicly restrain you unless you make it necessary."

I CAN FEEL Father standing right behind me. I don't know if that is to show his support or to remind me not to flee. The second I see the ship waiting to take me planetside, my hands begin to mist. I can't believe I am allowing them to do this to me. The moment I hesitate to step forward they all draw their weapons, and I can't help but laugh, because I know none of them would be able to hold me, but one word stops me.

"SON?"

I HEAR the question in Father's voice, and I know this is about more than myself. If I flee now, not only will I lose Jade, but he will have to hunt me to the ends of this universe, as he has given his word I would cooperate. It was much easier when I was alone. I didn't have these thoughts of compromise or consequences.

. . .

Before I realize what I am doing, I am ducking into the prisoner transport, leaving all that I have ever cared about behind.

Chapter Twenty-Seven

Jade

I ᴋɴᴏᴡ the moment he leaves the ship, because I can feel our link weaken. The big guy who has been holding me must have felt the fight leave me because he sits me down. I turn ready to give him a piece of my mind only to be stunned by what I am seeing. "You have wings?"

"Vᴇʀʏ ᴏʙsᴇʀᴠᴀɴᴛ ᴏғ ʏᴏᴜ, little female. I don't think we have been properly introduced. I am RaZ and this big green fellow behind me is XuL. You will be staying with us and our mates until the trial is over."

· · ·

"But you have wings and fangs. Are you like me?"

"We are the same, but different. However, you have much more in common with my mate Katherine and she is eagerly awaiting us planet side. Come, I have been away from my mate for way too long and I am in the need of her loving arms."

His words punch me right in my guts and he must have realized it immediately.

"Forgive me Jade, that come out wrong. The last thing any of us want is to make this harder on you. I know everything seems overwhelming and negative right now, but don't lose your faith. There are benefits to being a son of DaR. Our Father is a brilliant strategist and if this can be won, it will be."

I follow him down the long hallway numb to the things going on around me. The harsh looking one, I think he is called XuL, secures a set of straps over me in one of the seats on the shuttle. I nod my thanks and he pats me on the leg before turning away. I don't know why that simple act brings tears to my eyes. Maybe it was the kindness of a stranger or the fact that he looks harsh and mean, but his actions simply prove that he is more than his appearance.

It seems like I no more than blink when we land again. Unlatching the belts around me, I turn when I see the ramp opening on the side of the ship. Without thought, I start forward only for a large hand to grab me before I can step out. RaZ flares his wings out in front of me, blocking the sunlight.

"Woah, there little one, we don't know how you are going to react to Darverius' suns, so we need to take these first few steps cautiously."

Folding one wing in, he gently pulls me forward, covering all of my hand with his own but one fingertip. Hesitantly, he leans me towards the sun rays. After a few seconds, my skin starts to turn red like I am getting a bad sunburn, and I jerk back.

"The good news is you didn't internally combust. Bad news, you are going to have to stay out of the direct sun. I believe early morning or evening twilight you will do fine, but unless you want to look like a red Blood Beet quickly, you need to stay out of the sun. This rising you are a lucky female because you have me as an escort, and I am equipped with the best shelter available for sensitive little vampires like yourself. Step right on up here and snuggle in, little one, I will keep you safe until we get inside."

HATING the thought of anyone else holding me, and the fact that this guy smells bad, I make myself get close. RaZ puts an arm around my waist, holding me loosely as he stretches a wing up and over me, shading my entire body from the rays above as we quickly walk forward.

A DOOR SLIDES open in front of us, and the moment we are inside he lets go. The instant coolness the interior offers once inside is wonderful. I hear a squeal and the next second RaZ is wrapped around a small form that I cannot see, because his wings are surrounding them both in privacy.

A FEMALE'S voice has me turning, "Forgive the children, they tend to forget they are in the public often. Katherine and RaZ are not fans of being away from each other for long, as you can see."

. . .

"Oh, my God you are beautiful."

"Well, thank you, but you are not too shabby yourself. I'm Victoria, by the way. The set of legs hanging out of those wings is Katherine. I am going to assume you are Jade?"

"Yes."

"You might as well come on with me. Those two will be distracted for the next couple of hours. You will be staying with me and my mate Tyberius while the trial is going on."

"I don't want to put you out any. I am sure I can find lodging of my own."

"Nonsense, we have plenty of rooms and for now you are safer within these walls than anywhere else. Especially, since the men are tending to SiN. We have much to discuss, and right now the last thing you need is to be alone. RaZ was talking to Katherine this morning, and he said that you had just awakened, is that true?"

. . .

"YES, it's been a very trying day."

"YOU ARE BEING humble when you say that, Jade. I personally have never been through an awakening. I was born a Vampire, but I can sympathize with the rest of it."

"YOU'RE A VAMPIRE?"

WHEN SHE SMILES AT ME, I see her fangs lengthen and then retract. "I am, and so is Katherine, RaZ, and my mate Tyberius. So you see, you are not alone. Come, let's spend the afternoon talking about men and drinking wine. SAGE has prepared some rather unique blends. I believe will be quite pleasurable to your palette and it will also help with the cravings."

"WILL I be able to see SiN later?"

"I WOULDN'T THINK so this soon. Tyberius is an Elder, but he only has so much pull. I know they are trying to keep this trial as private and quiet as possible, so only family members will be allowed to stand witness tomorrow."

. . .

THE EVENING BECOMES TRYING for me. All the voices start blurring together as the noise becomes so loud, I can't sort through them individually. Victoria must have noticed I was having a hard time, because she motions for me to get up and follow her.

"I AM SORRY, Jade I should have realized that all of this would be overwhelming to you, especially this soon. You have had no time to adjust to yourself let alone your surroundings. Things will get easier each day, I promise. This will be your room while you are staying with us. SAGE had CIP make you some clothing and I believe they are already in the closet. The adjoining bathroom is also all yours, so take a long hot bath and try to rest some. Tomorrow will be a long one."

"THANK YOU, Victoria, I appreciate you taking me in, being a complete stranger and all."

"SWEETHEART, you will learn quickly we take care of our own. I will send for you in the morning before we leave for the trial."

THE SILENCE once the door closes behind me is wonderful. I don't know how long I stand here, letting my mind quiet, but finally, I snap out of it and make my way towards the bathroom. That bath that Victoria mentioned sounds wonderful now.

TAKING A SECOND TO LOOK AROUND, I am shocked to see the main furniture seems to resemble antiques back home on Earth. There is a large sleigh bed in the center of the room, and it is covered in a pale green quilt with tons of different colored pillows. Doilies and fringed lamps sit on the stands on each side. The entire room has an old-world feel, like something you would see in a castle. The same look follows into the bathroom because right in the middle, sits a huge clawfoot tub.

THE WATER inside of it is steaming, so someone must have just filled it for me. Not willing to waste a minute of the heaven that awaits me. I strip quickly, then slowly enter the water. The moment I am settled in, I lean back and close my eyes. Immediately, reaching out towards SiN.

I CAN FEEL his restlessness and worry, but other than that he seems fine. I miss him, but I don't know if it is simply because he is familiar, or if it's this mate bond thing they have all been telling me about. The pull of sleep almost has me dozing off in the tub, so I make myself get out. Drying off quickly, I grab the first thing I see in one of the drawers and pull it over my head.

ONCE I MANAGE to make it to the bed, I am out, Then the dreams commence. Suddenly, I can feel the sting of a whip against my skin, then his maniacal laughter surrounds me. I scream out over and over again as each strike rips pieces of my flesh away. Every time I try to put a face onto the man doing this to me, the beatings become worse. I search for the meaning as to why he is treating me this way, but no answers come forth. He has become a faceless terror haunting me. Suddenly a voice calling out for me has me jerking straight up in the bed.

MY EYES open to find a pale green teenage girl leaning over me. She is unlike anything I have ever seen before and strangely beautiful in her own way. Long white, pink, and brown hair surrounds an angelic face. Large pink eyes swirl unworldly as I feel like she is seeing more than me lying here before her. She pushes me back down on the bed and wipes the tears from my face.

"SHUSH, you're ok. Your dreams woke me, I didn't mean to disturb you, but I quickly realized you couldn't get out of it, so

I started calling out for you. That bad man will never hurt you again, Jade, and I will make sure he never hurts another. That I promise you. In time, the dreams will cease, and the faceless male will no longer have a hold on your mind. Because you will know you are stronger than he is. Your inner strength is the one thing that has kept you alive, now your physical strength will complete you. You have prayed for peace your whole life, don't lose your faith now. Because it will be tested thoroughly before all things will be revealed."

"THANK YOU, I'm sorry … but grateful that you woke me up. Who are you?"

"MY NAME IS KEIDA, you know my dad, XuL."

"HE WAS VERY KIND to me. I can see that has rubbed off onto his daughter. However, I would have never dreamed you were his child."

SHE SMILES SWEETLY DOWN at me as she runs her small hand over my face, tracing my features. "My characteristics are similar to my mother's. You will meet her tomorrow; we didn't arrive until after you had already retired for the evening. Your mind is tired, and you need to rest. I will stay with you until you drift back off to sleep."

I START TO SAY SOMETHING, but she shakes her head no. The last thing I can remember is her touching my forehead.

Chapter Twenty-Eight

SiN

THIS HAS BEEN the longest night of my entire existence. I could feel Jade as she was trying to maneuver through her first rising yesterday. Her confusion and the need to escape were not much different from my own, but it was the nightmares. Then her screams had me practically tearing the walls down.

IF I HAD NOT FELT a calmness come over her shortly after they began. I am not sure I could have kept my word and not broken out of here. Several times through the night, Father checked on me and even brought me a few bags of that nasty stuff that I had to make myself ingest.

.   .   .

I HAVEN'T BEEN ALLOWED to speak to anyone since they brought me here, but it is easy to see the worry on Father's face the last time he came in. Even though I couldn't talk to him I know he has stayed near this whole time. I would have thought he would've wanted rid of me and all the problems I have caused. Having a father is confusing.

THE DOOR OPENS and two guards walk in. They motion for me to turn around and put my hands behind my back. One of them grabs me roughly, and just as he starts to put the cuffs on, Father's voice echoes throughout the room.

"I WOULD TAKE CARE, that is my son you are manhandling."

INSTANTLY, the male let go of me. He turns me around cuffing my hands in front instead, then motions for me to go ahead of them. I walk out with a grin on my face at the feeble attempt they have made to contain me. Father has to know I can easily break these cuffs, but he still let them use these. *Is he testing me?*

I SMELL her before I even step into the room, and my head turns immediately, searching for her. Two other females stand beside Jade, and I can tell she is struggling not to run to me. But the moment I smile at her, she relaxes, and I am shocked when she blows me a kiss. Distracted by Jade, I almost forgot where I am, until a powerful voice echoes through the room.

"SIN, the last remaining heir to family Yamamura, son of Commander DaR, and Grandson to Elder Tyberius. You have been brought before this council to answer for the crimes and charges that have been recorded against you. At this time, how do you plead?"

"GUILTY."

"WELL, this was quicker than I anticipated. With that plea, you will be sentenced to death next rising."

THE ENTIRE ROOM explodes into chaos. I can hear Jade screaming out my name, and I have to make myself remain standing here.

MY GRANDFATHER TYBERIUS is instantly on his feet. "I overrule that sentencing for the simple reason he is now life-bound to another. If he is sentenced to death, then she will be also, and she is innocent in all of this. The case will be heard in its entirety before any rulings will be made or I will step down from my seat on this council."

"Elder Tyberius, we understand that you have a personal interest in this subject and therefore cannot look at this subjectively, but because of the nature of the crimes, we will hear what he has to say for himself and the witnesses that have come forth. If at the end of this trial, he is still found guilty, you will abide by the final ruling of the Elders."

"I accept those terms."

"Then let's get on with it. The first thing on the docket is the most recent terrorist attack on our beloved Solanar and SCOUT. The recordings read that SiN set off the bomb that knocked SCOUT's main processor offline. He also took a human female that is under the personal protection of our own Commander DaR to be sold for credits. SiN, how do you plead?"

Before I can say a word, SCOUT appears in the room before me. "Elders, please excuse my sudden appearance, but I believe you have been misled with that information and I want to clear that record before it can go any further."

"Proceed, SCOUT, we are always willing to listen to your counsel."

"First of all, I want it to be recorded that I took it upon myself to act that rising. Commander DaR never gave me permission to engage in battle nor take this solid form. Because I acted out on my own by overriding the safety measures put in place to protect Solanar. A disaster almost destroyed all that we hold dear, but this male is not responsible for that, I am. The only thing he can be charged with is the intercepting of an unauthorized device from Jynrel Pirates who were trying to sell it on the illegal market. I believe it malfunctioned while he was opening the case."

"This does put a different perspective on this issue, SCOUT. This charge will be wiped from his records. I am assuming that this occurrence will never happen again?"

"I have taken precautions that cannot be manipulated. Solanar will never be vulnerable again."

. . .

"You are excused SCOUT and thank you for bringing this to our attention."

"I would like to remain as legal counsel for Master SiN if that is ok with the Elders?"

They all look at each other, then at me. "SiN, do you have a need for counsel?"

"I will not turn down his advice if allowed."

"SCOUT, you may proceed."

Before they can say another word, the side door opens, and in walks my aunt Serena. "Elders, I am here to represent my family and I would like to approach the bench if possible."

She smiles sadly, grazing my cheek lovingly with her hand as she walks past. I have to put my head down to hide the emotions rolling through me with her appearance. "My name is Mistress Serena, oldest daughter of the Yamamura family. Here is the birth certificate confirming that VilaSiN Yamamura is the last living male heir of our family line. I am here to offer a sponsorship for all his debts, and crimes intertwined with obtaining them."

"THIS IS HIGHLY UNLIKELY, Mistress Serena, before we could even consider granting this. We would have to know the amount he owes, due to the crimes that were obtained."

THE ELDER STARTS LOOKING through the Holo pad only to throw it down. "Does anyone know why there are no currency amounts listed below any of these stated crimes?"

SCOUT SPEAKS UP, "Elder, it is possible that all debts have been paid or returned prior to this trial."

MY AUNT COMES to my side with a small smile on her face. "Mistress Serena, you have given us a legal birth record, but the name does not match the accused."

"THIS IS HIS PROPER NAME, one that has not been spoken to him until this date. It is one and the same."

. . .

"IT ALSO STATES HERE that you are his mother?"

"I AM HIS BIOLOGICAL MOTHER, but because of infertility problems, my sister carried him to term. Then she ran off with him, and his sister, hiding them before I could intervene. We have just recently been made aware of the things my sister did and blamed on VilaSiN."

THE ELDER ALMOST SEEMS AMUSED. "Lord of Light, this case is unraveling as we speak. We will keep your papers in mind, but we still have several other instances to report. The second charge is the impersonation of Commander DaR on Targres Four, where he not only took the entire funds from the Scientific Sector, he also openly fired upon General Tordan in a public market, endangering him and the pedestrians in the market."

FATHER STEPS IN. "If I may speak, Elders?"

"BY ALL MEANS, it seems to be an open floor this rising. Proceed Commander."

· · ·

"General Tordan and I were trying to undercover an underground militia that was attacking the Pleasure sector on Targres Four, but we couldn't get close. So we set up a fake market, hoping to draw them out with some well-spread rumors about some weapons that would be in the area. Since I couldn't be in two places at once. SiN acted in my place at the bank. Our cover was almost blown when the machine first denied his blood sample, but we easily deflected that as it was faulty, and this gave SiN time to use some of my own blood to use on the machine.

"The credits were paid back the same rising, but we couldn't take the chance of saying it wasn't SiN, as he had just made contact with their leaders. Tordan and I put on a nice show for the locals, but there was no danger of anyone being harmed."

"And General Tordan will verify all this?"

"Yes, he is currently on Falcor, but has forwarded a written statement to your Holo screen for verification."

"This charge will also be removed from his record. Third on the docket, I can't wait to see who is going to speak up for this one. It seems that SiN infiltrated not only your dwelling, Commander DaR, but also Falcor, attempting to take your mate each time."

"That is correct, but we were testing the safety precautions I had put in place to protect my mate and the other females in my care. Because of SiN's essence, he easily tricked the sensors, and both times was only inches from taking her. These tests gave us vital information about what security measures needed tightened up."

When Kira and the young human boy walk up, I about fall over. "Elders, if I may?"

"Don't be humble, Mistress Kira. Please come on up; everyone else has."

"Sir, I was not aware of the plans, nor the test DaR was analyzing and yes, both times SiN practically scared me to death. However, he never harmed me, but DaR sure felt my wrath afterward when he told me what they were doing."

"This explains you, Mistress Kira, what about the boy? I was informed that he is the only one in this room capable of holding SiN, or VilaSiN, as he is called to some."

. . .

"Sir, I was simply reacting to the circumstances. I believed Kira was truly in danger and acted without proper training. As you can see from the logs on Falcor, from that very moment, I have had a rigorous training schedule because of my actions."

"It seems as though that crime will also be taken from his file. The other charges are minor, and I am sure someone present would simply take credit for them as well if read.

"Commander, you should be a proud male. The unison of this family can not only be seen in the actions here today, but also in the unity standing side by side at the back of this court. We will convene for a short break, and I will come back to inform you of our final ruling. Someone take those cuffs off the male."

I finally let the breath out I was holding and turn around shocked to see the support standing in the room. Many of my brothers are standing arm in arm, nothing but a rainbow of colors here to support someone who has hated them because of who they were born to. Behind Jade stands a handful of Human females, also in every color, shape, and form.

. . .

"Before I can think any further, my aunt is standing before me. "Please forgive me, VilaSiN. I think … I always knew you were mine. I longed to hold you in my arms from the first moment I saw you. When I threatened to take you from her, she ran. By the time I found you again, she had already corrupted your small mind with her cruelty. I have wronged you in so many ways, but I promise no more. I am going to step out for a moment, your father wants to speak to you, but I will return shortly."

"How did you find out?"

"We will discuss that later, right now we just need to get you cleared and out of here."

The moment she steps away, a set of soft arms wrap around me. Lowering my head down, I bury my nose in Jade's soft hair. As I wrap myself around her, the world finally starts to make sense. All the questions of my childhood are finally being answered.

Chapter Twenty-Nine

KATHERINE

THIS ENTIRE RISING has been nothing but an emotional rollercoaster for everyone. I have done my best to not worry RaZ, but the mark on my hand is fading quickly. And I have even been hearing the insane laughter of the Soul Keeper in my dreams.

UNTIL THE MOMENT I lay eyes upon Serena, I have no idea how I am going to fulfill my side of this bargain. But when she came in announcing to the world that SiN was hers. I knew this was where Ellaria wanted to be. To make things right, she needs to be placed back where she was always meant to be. With her mother.

When Serena leaves the room with tears in her eyes, I follow her, watching as she walks into a public restroom. When I open the door, she is crying, standing at one of the sinks. "Forgive me, I will step out and give you some privacy. It's been a trying rising for me."

"No, you're fine. A lot has come out in the open today. You don't have to leave. If it's ok, I would love to talk to you for a few minutes. How did you find out SiN was your true son?"

"When they publicly announced SiN's incarceration, the doctor who helped my sister destroy our family came to me. You see, he assumed, if he told me his part in all of this, that I might give him credits to come before the Elders to verify that VilaSiN was really mine. He thought he could extort me and my family with the truth. I wanted to strangle him with my bare hands. If I could have resurrected my sister, it would be me in there instead of SiN standing trial for murder. Lord of Light, how I failed him.

. . .

"THE SAD PART is this is all on me. I couldn't stand to look at SiN. I loved … love DaR so much that the very sight of that child simply reminded me of what I had lost. Now don't get me wrong, I have a good mate. He is all that I should have ever wanted in a male, but DaR was my first love and the way things happened between us, well, there was no fixing it."

"ARE you going to tell him the truth?"

"No, why should I allow her to hurt him further? Right now, he probably thinks I made all of this up just to save SiN. I felt mine and DaR's bond break the moment he held his Kira in his arms. She was able to grant him the happiness I never could. Do I hate her for it? A little, but I am grateful too. Because when the bond broke, it allowed me to finally see my own mate with fresh eyes and our relationship has been improving ever since.

"DaR NOW RECOGNIZES SiN as his son, and in the long run, that's all that matters. I have no idea why I am opening up to you like this. I am just so lost. Until that male confessed his part in all of this, I didn't even know there was another child. I had a daughter and had no idea. I let her die! Because I was so wrapped up in my own misery."

. . .

HER TEARS TUG at my heart, and I walk over, gently pulling her into my arms. The moment my hand touches her back, I feel Ellaria leave me, implant herself back into her mother. *What was once broken has now been healed.* I hear the words of the Keeper of Souls in my mind, and I know that he no longer has a hold on me.

"SERENA, if you ever need anyone to talk to, my name is Katherine. I live in the Dark Forest with my mate RaZ, but we come to Solanar regularly because of family living in SCOUT's main building complex."

"DaR'S FATHER?"

"YES."

"IT ALMOST KILLED DaR, losing his father. I am glad that all his faith is finally coming full circle. I should get back; I thank you more than you know for your kindness. Somehow, I feel now like this will all work out."

AS SHE IS WALKING out the door, I stop her. "If by chance you ever find yourself with child one rising and it's a girl, I hear the name Ellaria is quite beautiful."

"WHY YES, it is. I will keep that in mind."

THE DOOR OPENS and in walks Kira. She stops in her tracks, looking first at Serena and then me. They don't say a word to each other. The one who lost and the one who holds the love of the same man.

SERENA NODS her head and then walks out the door. Kira stands there a moment before walking in, checking her hair in the mirror. "Katherine, you don't have to say anything, yes, she is stunning. Damn that woman, with all that pretty blue skin, and those markings. She just reeks with that sweet and innocent act of hers."

"YOU DIDN'T SEEM TOO happy to finally put a face with a name."

"HOW WOULD you feel if the woman RaZ loved before you walked in looking like that?"

. . .

"POINT TAKEN."

"KIRA, you know she seemed pretty miserable."

"I WANTED to rip her arms off when she went to stand beside DaR."

"YEAH, but he only had eyes for you, her hold was broken years ago."

"OH, I know, but let me be petty for just a minute, then I promise I'll be good. Why couldn't she have been old and wrinkled?"

"JEALOUSY IS NOT a good shade on you, Kira."

"OH, HUSH."

GRABBING HER ARM, both of us laugh as we walk out of the bathroom together.

Chapter Thirty

SiN

WHEN THE ELDERS come back into the room, everyone returns to where they were. By the looks on some of the Elders' faces, I have a very uncomfortable feeling about what they are going to say.

"VILASIN YAMAMURA, as we have read over your file there are several other instances that were brought to our attention. One is the attempted kidnapping of the human female; another is the smuggling of weapons and research. We could charge you for these actions, but we propose another option instead. If you refuse this offer, you will be sentenced to serve twenty Orbital rotations in the maximum-security prison located on the Alkata Moon."

Gasps come from where the human females are standing, and I can feel Jade's terror through our link.

"I am listening."

"All charges will be dropped, and you will have full funding directly from us to simply continue doing what it seems you do best. We need someone who can infiltrate the outer sector and the criminal actions going on there. Recently your father Commander DaR has brought it to our attention that Commander ZoD could possibly be at the head of these criminal acts.

"We have seen the footage of the facility he is overseeing and how he personally took one of the Human Females against her will. He is not above our reign and will have to answer for his crimes as you have, but we need more evidence in order to get the charges to stick. I don't believe he will have quite the support you have had in this trial. Before we can formally charge a Commander, there can be no shadow of a doubt.

. . .

"RIGHT NOW, you still have personal contacts with the Jynrel, Korgons, and the Waldron. You can walk freely among them because they think you are trying to destroy your family and will use any means to do so. We want you to use your reputation to help us bring down these factions."

MY FIRST THOUGHTS are of Jade. "You are aware that I am a fully mated male."

"YES, we have been informed of that. The Elders thought we would help spread the rumor that you stole her and turned her against her will. We could even say that she is trying to escape you."

"I WOULD STILL BE HUNTED. Maybe that's not the life I want for myself or my mate any longer."

"I AM sure the Commander could provide you with a code that would allow you to enter and exit Darverius space without anyone knowing. Your family has a strong presence on several planets in this sector. If things become too dangerous or your cover is blown, there will be plenty of places for you to hide out."

.   .   .

"THE ENTIRE UNIVERSE knows why I have been brought here today. How are you going to explain me simply walking away."

"THAT'S AN EASY ONE. You are going to escape with your mate, and we are going to make it look like the entire fleet is chasing you. However, we lose you in that magic shuttle of yours."

"CAN I have a minute to talk to the Commander about this?"

"BY ALL MEANS."

"FATHER?"

"I NEVER THOUGHT of this option, but SiN, it could work. Between SoL and SCOUT, we could monitor your location at all times. We can even discuss a few of your brothers being stationed close to you in case you need immediate help or a distraction. You will not be alone out there; we will discuss each and every mission before you head in. So it's not going to be exactly what you have been doing up to date."

· · ·

"What about Jade? I won't leave her."

"Your enemies will underestimate her. She will be your best kept secret weapon if this adventure is something she wants to participate in with you. Your mate can start training with Keida and Zura. You could put off leaving until you are comfortable with her being able to defend herself."

I nod my head then turn back to the Elders who have been listening to all of this. "One more moment, please." I motion for Jade to come to me, and she rushes over. "What do you think of this plan?"

"As long as we're together, we will figure it out." She walks away from me, and right up to the Elders. "How long would we have? I am new to this world and the changes that I have been through."

"The rumor could be leaked out that SiN is in hiding, trying to let things settle down some after escaping from this chamber and stealing you."

. . .

SHE WALKS BACK over to me taking my large hand in her smaller one. I bring it up to my lips. Kissing her hand gently. The smell and feel of her veins pulsing under her thin skin causes my fangs to lengthen.

"ELDERS, it looks like you have yourselves a set of spies. Now if you don't mind, I need to take my mate and escape. Father, we will be in touch in a couple risings." I lean down, pulling Jade closer. "Where would you like to go my love?"

"LET'S GO HOME. To the one who took us when no one else would."

"AS YOU WISH. But let's make this look good."

THROWING JADE OVER MY SHOULDER, and with a mere thought, I mist us out of the building. I can hear alarms and guards running behind us in vain. Our laughter is the last thing they hear as I lead them on a merry chase through the corridors of Solanar.

Chapter Thirty-One

DaR

PUTTING my head down to hide the smile on my face. I look up at my own Father only to see he is also having a hard time keeping a straight face as SiN's laughter echoes throughout the room.

I START towards Kira when another small hand stops me. "DaR, can I speak with you for a moment?"

GLANCING over to where Kira is standing, I see her stop when she sees Serena's hand on my arm. I motion for her to come to me and the smile she grants me lightens the heaviness this day has placed on my heart.

TUCKING KIRA UNDER MY ARM, I turn my attention back towards Serena. Finally, seeing the female I had loved for so many rotations … differently. Serena looks down at Kira, as she is substantially taller than my little mate, then back up to me.

"TO BE SO small they make a big impression, don't they?"

SMILING, I kiss the top of Kira's head as she stands here, supporting me without saying a word.

"DaR, first of all, I want to apologize. Part if not all of this is my fault. I should have told you the moment Semora found out she was carrying your child. However, I was in denial and was convinced she was lying just to hurt me further. I have no idea what I did to make her hate me so, but she destroyed … well she definitely made her mark on all of our lives. The moment I held VilaSiN in my arms I knew he was yours. All I did after that was make up excuses in my head as to why I shouldn't tell you.

· · ·

"YOU HAD JUST WON the Commander trials, and your father was missing. When I left the planet, it was easier to push all of this and the circumstances to the back of my mind. Then my father became sick, and I returned, only to find out that you were raising XuL, and RaZ on your own. I kept telling myself that I could find a way to fix all of this, but I was a coward. All this pain could have been prevented, not just for VilaSiN, but for you too.

"SIMPLY, I wanted to say I am sorry. I have already spoken to VilaSiN, and I will be an active part of his life from now on, one way or another."

IT'S easy to see the sincerity on her face, but I still wonder. "Serena, why did you tell the Elders you were his mother?"

SHE LOOKS DOWN AT KIRA, an unknown message is sent between them that I don't understand. When she looks back at me, I can tell immediately that she is going to lie.

"I THOUGHT the paperwork would be more convincing if the one presenting it was directly affected."

. . .

FOR ONE MOMENT, I ponder on the fact that if she had been his mother how I would feel about it. If it had been before My Kira, it might have changed things, but the Lord of Light had another path I needed to walk.

"I APPRECIATE you telling me your side, Serena. Now if you will excuse us, I have been away from my mate for too many rotations now. This trial and all its manipulating has worn this old male out and I am in need of a nice vacation."

SHE SMILES SADLY, then turns away, walking alone out of the room.

I PULL MY KIRA CLOSE. "You wanna go out on a date?"

"AREN'T we doing that a little backward, love?"

"NAHH, OUR WORLD, OUR RULES."

Chapter Thirty-Two

SiN

I REMATERIALIZE at the base of Mystic. Pulling Jade around in front of me, her laughter fills my heart. Right at this moment, it dawns on me how much this little female has changed my course in just a few risings.

A LARGE LIMB LOWERS DOWN, lifting me and Jade up simultaneously. Returning both of us to the only place that has ever felt like home, Mystic's sanctuary. The moment we are safely inside, Jade runs over to one of the walls and spreads her arms out, hugging it. "Oh Mystic, I didn't think I would ever grace these walls again."

．　．　．

A SMALL LIMB comes out circling Jade's waist and I know this is simply Mystic's way of hugging her back. Her deep voice echoes throughout the small opening.

"SiN, Jade, it pleases these old roots that you have returned to me. It has been way too quiet with the two of you gone. I can see there has been a few minor changes in you both. SiN, is that a smile gracing your usually sour face?"

I TRY to sober up quickly only to start laughing again when Jade rolls her eyes. "Yes, Mystic that is a smile, they are becoming a bad habit lately. This little minx has bewitched me with humor and happiness."

"THE LORD OF LIGHT has answered my prayers, after all. I have spent many risings praying for some light to be cast into your darkness SiN, and it pleases me to see this bond between you two. The supplies Katherine's hounds brought are still in the trunks next to the wall, and I am not too old to realize you two need some quality time together. So, I am going to return to my roots for the rest of this rising. I have a couple of saplings I need to tend to."

．　．　．

THE MOMENT MYSTIC LEAVES, Jade takes a deep breath and I can tell all of a sudden, she doesn't know what to say.

"HEY PRETTY GIRL, you need a snack? I hear there is a male around here who likes to be chewed on by curvy little females."

HER GIGGLE LIGHTENS MY HEART. "Do you now. I just might know a girl like that, but she doesn't just chew on anybody. He has to be pretty convincing in order to lure her in."

"REALLY, hum, let me think on this some. You see, I don't know this female well, but I hear she is a real keeper."

"WHAT MAKES YOU THINK THAT?"

"OH, let me see. The fact that she is willing to run away with me and be a fugitive for the rest of her existence is pretty convincing."

"MAYBE SHE JUST THINKS YOU'RE hot and you smell good. A girl could do worse you know."

. . .

I HAVE her in my arms before she can blink, twirling her around playfully. She runs her finger through my hair, tilting my head back. "What does a male have to do to earn a kiss around here?"

"HAVE YOU BEEN GOOD TODAY?"

"NOT IN THE SLIGHTEST."

HER MOUTH IS on mine instantly, and everything in my world is finally complete. If someone had told me rotations ago, I would be where I am this rising. I probably would have mocked them for a fool. Isn't it amazing the path we are sent on during this walk of life?

Chapter Thirty-Three

Jade

A WHIRLWIND. That's what the last few days have been. Nothing but nonstop up and down emotions. I have been thrown away, chased, sold, experimented on, and then turned into a mythical creature. But if this has all been a dream, just leave me alone because I think I am about to get to the hottest part yet.

I KNEW the first time I laid eyes on SiN my life was going to change, but no part of my imagination could have dreamed this up. My hands run over every inch of his sculpted body. I feel small in his large arms and because of our link, I can tell he is enjoying this as much as I am. His emotions and senses are so intertwined with my own that I don't know if I am experiencing my pleasure or his.

HE SLIDES an arm snuggly around me, pulling me tighter against him. His warm breath tickles my shoulder as he moves my hair out of the way. Soft lips nuzzle my throat and I squirm against him as he teases me with the scrape of his fangs against my skin. When he finally gives me what I need when I feel his fangs sink deep. I moan out as my body seeks the release only he can give me.

MY EYES practically roll back in my head as I feel my desire damping the panties I have on. Hating the feel of the barriers between us, I tear at the clothing we have on and within seconds. I have our clothes in shreds and his massive shaft in hand.

EVERY PULL from my neck makes me crave him that much harder. He releases me, licking the puncture wounds until the bleeding stops and I almost attack him in my fevered desire. Climbing up his immense body I kiss him aggressively, our fangs clack together and the taste of our combined blood just spurs me on.

. . .

I WRENCH my mouth from his, biting him right above his nipple. Working his shaft forcefully with my hand as I take what I need. His hands feel like fire against my cooler flesh, as they are everywhere all at once. He grips my breast, kneading them both at once and I arch into him craving more.

MY INSIDES ACHE for him and I almost collapse from pleasure when he finally inserts two fingers inside of me. He works my body as violently as I do his, both of us reaching for something just out of reach.

WITHOUT ANOTHER THOUGHT, I pull my fangs from his tender skin, making sure to lick the wounds I made, as I don't want to waste a drop of the nectar his body produces. Climbing up higher I almost moan out in distress when he removes his fingers from my tender folds only to grip both of my butt cheeks as he lifts me up.

HE PEERS DOWN at my face as I slowly lower myself upon him, finally giving what I have been craving the most. The moment I have reached all my body can take, he takes over. His massive arms flex as he moves me up and down. My breast bouncing against his chest only adds to the stimulation he is putting me through. Over stimulated, all I can do is enjoy the ride.

. . .

BLINKING, I somehow, I find myself on my back with his wide shoulders between my thighs. Looking down, all I can see is a mischievous grin on his face before he licks my pleasure nub slowly. The heat building inside of me is so intense that tears form in my eyes. No one has ever made me feel this way. I lose all rational thoughts when suddenly everything seems to explode inside of me. I scream out his name as he thrust himself back inside of me.

CLOSING MY EYES, I savor every inch of him that has me filled to the point of pain being the pleasure. Holding my hips up, he moves me back and forth, a look of total bliss on his face as he races us both towards the same thing.

I CAN FEEL him lowering his hand, and the moment he touches my pleasure button. Reality leaves me, and I scream out so loud, I know the entire forest hears me. My inner walls milking him has SiN roaring and I swear for a moment his entire body gets larger.

SHIVERING from the intensity of it all. He looks down at me and we both start giggling when he says, "Frack, it's hot in here."

. . .

OUR COMBINED LAUGHTER echoes out through the forest as I pull him down on top of me.

"DID I HURT YOU?"

"MAYBE RIGHT HERE," I point at my right breast, "And right here, too. We may have to play doctor where you have to inspect me for injuries."

"IS THAT RIGHT, well how are you planning on paying for my services?"

"WE COULD WORK it out in trade."

"MISTRESS JADE, I think you are a woman after my heart."

"THAT'S a good thing because the moment I steal it from you. I am never giving it back. SiN, do you think it will always be like this?"

. . .

"I've heard that time only makes it that much sweeter."

Chapter Thirty-Four

SiN

Waking up with Jade in my arms, and the world around me quiet, is odd. I have spent so much time alone. My heart had filled full of hatred. Every waking moment of my life was used to figure out my next step in their ruination. Right now, I am on unfamiliar ground.

So many new experiences await on this new path I'm on, including this one. I can't help but smile as I try to untangle myself from her hair without waking her up. Scooting away from her, I tuck the blanket back around her. Walking over to the edge of the opening, I sit down, looking out over the dark forest below. I have spent many risings in this exact spot, but I have never seen it like this.

A LIGHT FOG has settled among the trees, hiding the forest floor from sight. The wind is calm and everything feels peaceful. That in itself is a new emotion for me. There seems to be a lot of firsts for me lately. Change is always hard, but I feel like I have wasted so many risings, now that I am finally seeing things clearer. The path of destruction I have left is easy to follow. Most of the things I have done, I don't know how to rectify, but first things first. I owe Mystic something.

"GOOD RISING MYSTIC," I whisper, trying not to wake Jade up.

"SIN."

"MYSTIC, I want to say thank you, and I am sorry all at once. I owe everything to you, even her."

"SIN, the first time I saw you stumbling along in the forest. I knew even though you were draped in darkness. There was a light within your soul that refused to be vanquished. Several times, I thought you would be lost to your hatred, but that light never went out. The youngling you were then needed me, and as you grew, the male you had become was still that same lost youngling watching the world continue on without him.

"YOU WERE nothing more than a sapling I was trying to mold until your trunk became strong enough to support the weight bearing down upon you. I am proud of the male you have chosen to be, and my part in it. As for the female, the Lord of Light gave her to you when you were at your darkest point. You were handed the tools you would need to change, it was simply up to you to do it."

THE BLACK MARK running up my arm starts to itch and I scratch at it vigorously. I swear, it looks like another sprout has grown further, almost to the point it's touching my neck.

"SIN, quit rubbing your arm, it will stop in time."

"IT'S DRIVING ME CRAZY. Do you know what this is?"

. . .

"Of course I know, I put it there. With a little help from your Father's Symbots."

"Are you going to tell me, or am I going to have to drag it out of you."

The entire tree moves slightly when she goes to laughing. "Little males, all of you are so impatient. Not including full of yourselves. How exactly are you planning on making me tell you?"

"Ugh, well … ok. You've made your point, now what's this thing crawling up my arm."

"It's the mark of the Guardians. No matter the planet, or where you are. If you are in need, they will come. It's the one and only gift I could bestow upon you to keep you safe as your travels take you far from me. You will be in great peril on the missions the Elders are sending you on, and because I am tied to Darverius, my reach only goes so far.

. . .

"THERE ARE GUARDIANS, however, on every habitable planet in this part of the universe. If there is ever a time you are in grave danger one will come to you."

"How?"

"THAT'S where the Symbots come in. Anytime you set foot on a planet they will notify every Guardian in the area of your arrival. You will be monitored at all times. You will never be alone again. That's why that fake mark was removed from your skin. No other markings will ever be needed by you. Because even a House Mark is not more powerful than a Guardians. In the history of our world, only four others have been chosen to wear the mark, it's a great honor."

"MYSTIC, I don't know what to say. I definitely don't deserve this."

"WHY IS THAT?"

"WELL. I am just me. Most of the time, I suck."

. . .

"TRUE, but I love you like I sprouted you myself. I know you will make me proud, because I already am. You could have stayed on your path of destruction SiN, and you had every right to feel the way you did. However, on the very rising, you realized how you had been manipulated. You mentally became who you were always meant to be, VilaSiN. You and Jade will go on many adventures together, and I will eagerly await the stories you have to tell me when you return home."

"WHAT ABOUT JADE, will the Guardians watch over her too?"

"GO LOOK on the inside of her right wrist."

WITH A THOUGHT, I am at her side. Gently, I turn her wrist over only to find a small mark in the shape of a tree. "In her world, they were called Life Trees, and I thought that mark would be appropriate. No one will know it for anything other than a human tattoo. Go live the life the Lord of Light has given you to the fullest SiN. Enjoy the arguments as much as you enjoy the laughter. I am sure you will have plenty of both.

"YOUR FATHER HAS BEEN WALKING the Dark Forest since early rising. You may want to go speak with him while your mate slumbers. The changes to her human body will require her to rest more than yours do. I will watch over her while you go to him."

"WHERE IS HE NOW?"

"HEAD TOWARDS YOUR SHUTTLE."

Chapter Thirty-Five

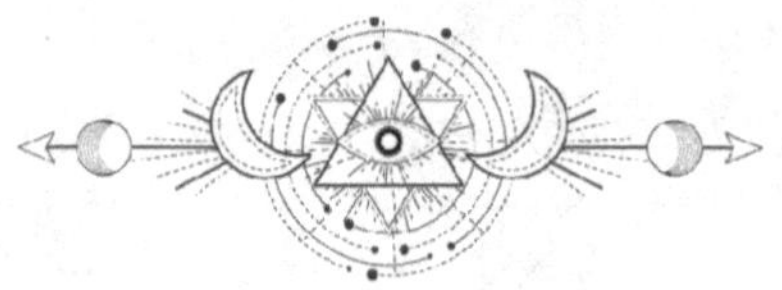

SiN

Misting through the forest, Father is easy to detect.
When I appear only a few steps behind. He turns, drawing his
ax ready to fight, until he sees it's me.

"Don't put it down old man, let's see what you've got."

"As much as it would delight me to put you in your place,
youngling. Unfortunately, we have matters that need to be
attended to, but now that the challenge has been issued there

will be a rising, I will test your skills. You can count on that. Tordan is on his way down to retrieve your shuttle."

"On whose authority?"

"The Elders. Now, before you allow your anger to override your senses. I was discussing the circumstances of the trial with Tordan and we decided to use the credits the Elders have approved for you, to your advantage. However, since I don't know the location of your shuttle, I couldn't proceed without you."

"You mean the old mighty DaR was outsmarted by little old me?"

He stops mid-stride and looks up at the sky. "Twenty-three of them and I swear they all act the same. What have I done in this lifetime to deserve such disrespect from my own spawn?

"Boy, I brought you into this world and I can take you out of it. As a matter of fact, I truly believe if there was a lower number of all you boys … my life would be much calmer. So go ahead and put your name on the list of the ones I need to knock down a few notches."

I HAVE to bite my lip to keep from laughing at the expression on his face. "Come on, we don't want to get you too worked up with your failing health, old man. My shuttle is right over here." The second my shuttle recognizes my presence it appears in the field. Father whistles appreciably.

"Now, I see why you have her hid, that's a beauty. Where did you obtain it?"

"SHE IS A CUSTOM JOB. I had her special ordered and built on Skathi. She has saved my ass a million times."

"WHAT ABOUT WEAPONS?"

"YEAH, that is not a strong point. It has the mechanics and the wiring, but I didn't have the funds to get her armed. The interior is rather plain also, and there is no medical unit even though I designed a room for one."

. . .

"Does she have a name?"

"The Rambler."

"How do you feel about Tordan and SoL tuning her up a little."

"I am all for it, as long as SoL doesn't make it fu-fu, like the Explorer. Now, don't get me wrong, there are some serious luxuries on that ship, but it is a little over the top."

"I will pass that message on. When are you planning on starting Jade's training?"

"I would put it off forever if I could, but I know the Elders are not going to wait that long. If she is up to it, maybe I'll have her start watching them this rising."

"When I return to the dwelling, I will inform Kira. She is always excited to meet any of the new humans that keep popping up."

. . .

"I NEED TO GO. I can feel Jade awakening. Especially right now, I dislike leaving her alone. These changes are a lot harder on their species than ours. I will leave the shuttle open and unlock the safety measures so that Tordan can take it without any issues. We will join you later on this rising."

Chapter Thirty-Six

SiN

"Hey beautiful, I see you're up?"

"Yes, I didn't like waking up alone, don't make that a habit."

"I didn't want to wake you, one of us needs their beauty sleep and I had to meet Father. How are you feeling?"

"Aware, if that makes any sense."

. . .

"WE GOT a little sidetracked after the hearing last rising. Are you really ok with this scheme they have come up with? Because if you're not, you know hiding in plain sight is a gift of mine and we can simply disappear."

"YOU HAVE DONE ENOUGH RUNNING in your life. Let's use those ingenious skills of yours for a better use. There are others out there like me, SiN, and if I can help save one, I'm game."

"JADE, I won't set foot in that shuttle until I'm sure you can defend yourself. The thought of something happening to you because I was too slow to get there is unacceptable to me."

"SiN, I completely agree with you. I know I'm not ready. If only that was the sole thing I needed to adjust to. I can feel all this power in me, but I don't know what to do with it."

"A LITTLE EXCESS ENERGY, huh. Well, let's see if we can wear you down a little. I'm feeling a slight bit peaked, and I think I may need a snack. You are my favorite food at the moment. We have some time before we need to meet the others. Speaking of exploring, I don't think I have truly examined you yet, and you did say we was going to play doctor."

· · ·

TIME FLIES when you're having fun and it seems like I blink an eye and the main sun's are settling. Walking out of the Dark Forest hand in hand, we approach the main family dwelling together. Before we can even step onto the grass, we are surrounded by the Seline. Their growls and dripping fangs stop us in our tracks. A sharp whistle has them falling back as a small figure appears riding upon one.

"KEIDA, sweetness, you about scared me to death. Are you safe on … well that? It sure has a lot of teeth."

"JADE, this is SeeSee, he looks mean, but I promise it's all an act. Rub his belly and he will love you forever. Sorry, I wasn't out here when you guys first came through the forest. The Seline can be a little overprotective when it comes to us. They know your scents now, so you don't have anything else to worry about.

"I HEAR you are going to be my new sparring partner, Jade. It's so much fun once you get the hang of it. Unka SoL just brought me two new swords, but I am not allowed to use them while practicing yet. Come on, you can wear some of my old protective gear and I have a sword, I think will fit you perfectly. Before we can go play, Mom and Kira want to talk to you first. They are waiting in the Atrium, if you want to go on, you can't miss it. I need to talk to Unkle SiN for a second."

JADE LOOKS up at me and I motion for her to go on when I see the other two females coming this way. Keida and I both watch her walk off. "What can I do for you, little female? I see I didn't get the honorary title of Unka."

"THAT IS a title that must be earned. However, if what I am about to show you is taken care of properly, it will earn you that particular claim. I gained this information straight from Jade, as her dreams were haunted by his face. I took the face and the memories away from her, but I believe you will find this quite educational."

THE MOMENT she touches my forehead I am whirling through the mind and the torment of another, my Jade. Reliving each strike, and every burn, like they are happening to me instead of her. The maniacal laughter has me searching for the person who inflicted all this pain. The moment I see his face, my own anger takes over.

. . .

OPENING MY EYES. Keida's pink eyes swirl in anger. "Now Unkle SiN, go do what you do best. I will entertain your Jade until this task is complete. He is residing in an underground bunker near your Mother's home in District Seven. All you need to know I have shown you. Oh, one other thing. Unless you want her to feel what you're doing, you might want to block that link you two have. Or we won't be able to hold her here."

"KEIDA, SHE HAS BEEN THROUGH ENOUGH."

"THAT IS one thing we both agree on."

I LEAVE IMMEDIATELY, finding his location almost too easily. Opening the door, I am not shocked to find him gone as his scent is fading, but as I look around, I can tell he will return. So I sit down and make myself comfortable. It didn't take long for the door to open. The look on his face is priceless when he sees me sitting in the corner.

"COMMANDER, forgive me. I wasn't aware you were going to call upon me this rising. I would have been here to greet you, if I had."

. . .

STANDING UP SLOWLY, I smile at him. My hands itch, as I anticipate the amount of pain, I will unleash upon this male.

"YOU ARE NOT THE COMMANDER, are you?"

"WHAT GAVE IT AWAY? Don't you recognize your own work? After all, you are the reason I am breathing this rising. If not for your knowledge, I just might have been wiped off with a random cloth, but you came up with this ingenious plan. And Tada here I am. I am not sure if I should thank you or tear you to pieces."

HE HOLDS his hand out like that is going to stop me. "I should have known your aunt would run straight to you and tell you that ridiculous story."

"YOU MEAN MY MOTHER. The one you thought you could gain some credits from, by extorting her with this information. No, as much as you want to blame this on others, it was not her that showed me your face, it was my mate."

"YOU MUST BE MISTAKEN. I have no knowledge of your mate."

. . .

"Let me refresh your memory. She stands about this tall, has long black hair, and extremely rare violet eyes. From my understanding, she was in your care for quite some time until you became frightened her species might be found in your residence. I wonder, did it make you feel like a big male when you were stripping the tender flesh from her body? Or beating and burning her for your friends' entertainment. Did starving her get you off?"

"I told those idiots that memory block wouldn't hold and that we should just kill her."

"Oh, it held. She still can't remember anything before she was dumped into the forest. At this time, you are a faceless male who haunts her dreams occasionally. But we never really escape our sins do we, and one of yours is standing before you.

"You see, when a mate bond is formed, the information just flows back and forth between them. Right now, I am having a hard time blocking her from knowing what I plan on doing to you. You see, you not only stole me from my mother, but you also destroyed my life and then beat my mate within an inch of hers. So I think you and me have a little problem."

• • •

THE CLAWS on my hands extend just as he runs for the door. Instantly, I am in front of him, grabbing his head and I throw him against the door. Then taking a single finger, I cut open his cheek in the same manner he did Jades.

THE NEXT FEW hours I spend playing with him. Tearing him to pieces a little at a time, just as he did Jade. His screams echo throughout the room, but no one comes to his aid. My only thought is that SCOUT must be dampening the sounds in this area as he watches from some unknown location. The male's heart stops too soon and I watch as he bleeds out. I am disappointed that I couldn't make it last longer, but the worry I start to feel in my link to Jade has me realizing I have been gone long enough.

SCOUT APPEARS JUST as he takes his last breath. "I was studying your very unique techniques, and I found them quite educational, SiN. Now let me show you a little trick of mine."

HE FLICKS HIS FINGER, and a bubble surrounds what is left of the male. I actually jerk back when the inside of the bubble combust, disintegrating the body inside instantly. When it pops, there is nothing left but a few ashes.

. . .

SCOUT smiles as his form starts to fade. "I will put his name on the missing persons list. It was nice working with you SiN, reach out anytime you do something like this again. After all, what better way for me to learn than hands-on? You should return to your mate."

"Best idea I have heard all day."

Epilogue

SEVERAL ROTATIONS HAVE PASSED, and just like I predicted, the Elders became impatient. I stand around watching Jade as she hugs Keida and Katherine bye.

FATHER'S VOICE catches my attention. "The shuttle is ready to go, looks like they're loading the last of it now. Between the upgrades and its cloaking device, she should perform beautifully out there. How does it feel knowing you have the rest of your life ahead of you without all the weight of your past?"

"I DON'T KNOW how to put it in words, but I plan on figuring it out."

. . .

"SIN, your little mate has proven to be quite deadly. Keida is going to miss her. They have gotten close these last risings. I saw her surprise Katherine earlier, and no one, not even RaZ has ever been able to do that. Katherine is wicked fast, but Jade kept her on her toes."

"YEAH, she is pretty extraordinary, but to be mine, she would have to be."

FATHER LAUGHS, shaking his head. He reaches over, pulls me into him, and hugs me close. "I am proud of ya, Son. Now go do what you do best, but remember you are not alone out there. If a time comes and you need me, all you have to do is call out. If we lose contact with you or you come up missing, you sit tight. I will come for you."

JADE IS STANDING NEXT to me when he lets go, and I have to hide the tears that have formed. My entire life, I longed to hear those words out of his mouth. *Proud, and I will come for you.* Keida has even started calling me Unka. What more could a male possibly want in this world?

. . .

"WHEN YOU RETURN, we will have one of those family dinners Kira likes to plan. It would do you good to get to know your brothers better.

"AS LONG AS I am out on missions, Father. I won't endanger them, or your lives, but one rising I would like that."

TURNING TOWARDS JADE, "What do you say my little mate, you ready to chase the stars with me?"

SHE IMMEDIATELY STARTS TEASING ME. "You know, I don't really know you, and my parents taught me not to get in a car with strangers."

"WHAT'S TO KNOW? I am handsome, have great hands, and an outstanding sense of humor. I know how to do that thing with my tongue you like so well."

JADE SMACKS me on the arm playfully. "Stop it, someone will hear you. I can see humble is also on the list of your fine traits."

. . .

"Angel, I am anything you need or want me to be. I love you my violet-eyed savior."

"And I love you my humble, shy, ugly, and little helpless mate."

"Oh, you are going to pay for that."

Her laughter as I chase her up the ramp lightens my soul. I send a quick prayer up to the Lord of Light, thanking him for taking the chance on a sinner like me. May his light always shine strong, even in the darkest of times.

THE END

Other books from this Author:

<u>The Water Skippers series</u>

Water Skippers
(Kyle and Eden)
A Dragonfly's Whisper
(Nora and Roman)
Earth Shadow
(Lorene and Garret) part one
Shadow Reborn
(Garret and Lorene)
Petal
(Randy and Petal)
Miranda and the Dragonfly King
(Miranda and Tagon)

Water Skipper Series

Jennifer Julie Miller

The Forsaken series

The Forsaken series
Forsaken
(Lucas and Emma)
Betrayed
(Tavish and Eve)
Forgotten
(Tyberius and Victoria)
Spin off to DaR.

Darverius The house of DaR

Darverius, The House of DaR
DaR
(DaR and Kira)
XuL
(XuL and Brittany)
SoL
(SoL and Alana)
RaZ
(RaZ and Katherine)
A House of DaR Celebration (novella)
Tordan
(Tordan and Luna)
Hugo
(Hugo and Miya)
AvX

(AvX and Ivy)

SAGE (novella)
ViN
(ViN and Ember)

SCOUT (novella)
SiN
(SiN and Jade)

Note from the Author:

I hope... I have made you laugh, and possibly... even squeezed a few tears out of ya. Writing has been a lifelong dream for me, and our dreams are the only thing we have to build on!!!

So GO for it!!!!

Reading is a passion of mine as well. I believe there are Dragons, Unicorns, and multicolored Kitty Cats, because our imaginations are our own uniqueness.

I am thankful for the support of my family and friends.

To my readers, thank you for encouraging me to continue writing even though my worlds are a little different.

After all, I'm Appalachian, and I talk Appalachian. Therefore, I write Appalachian. All my books have country girls in them, and that's mainly because I only know how to speak country girl correctly.

Then to the Lord above, whose blessing gave a poor little girl from Ironton a chance to dream!

If you enjoyed this story, or any of my other ones, I ask that you take a few minutes of your time, and leave a review on Amazon, or Goodreads. It really helps new and older authors alike.

If you would like to stay in touch, hear about new releases, give some advice, or just drop a line. I love to talk books.

Contact the Author

You can find me on Facebook.

Https://facebook.com/JenniferJulieMiller.

On Twitter.

Https://www.twitter.com/jenniferrick

Or email me at:

Jenniferjuliemiller@gmail.com

Follow me on BookBub. **Https://www.bookbub.-com/profile/jennifer-julie-miller**

Follow me on Amazon.

Https://amazon.com/author/jjm5325903

And sign up for my email if you want to learn more about Darverius and DaR's twenty-two plus sons.

Https://eepurl.com/cfrL8X

DaR

Kira

In the blink of an eye, my whole world has collapsed around me. Headed towards my dream vacation, I was snatched right out of the air. My husband, the love of my life, was destroyed right in front of my eyes. He fought bravely, trying to protect me from a horror neither one of us could have ever imagined. I find myself standing in the spotlight on a stage. Mutilated and tortured, the blood from my body flowing freely down my legs along with my will to live. Piercing yellow eyes emerge from the darkness, but even the shadows can't hide his imposing form. Gentle, but terrifying arms reach out for me and within their embrace, can I find the will to live again?

DaR

I am a bad ass, known throughout the galaxy for my

brutality as a ruthless and feared commander. With that being said, somehow, I still got coerced into purchasing a slave. My eyes fall upon a small female whose very essence and eternal light is leaking out of her onto the floor below her. I watch in awe as she accepts her fate, willing her nightmare to be over. I almost turn away from her and the unnecessary cruelly in this room, but the very thought of her dying on that floor surrounded by the very monsters that have done this to her disgust me. I walk up among the beings surrounding her and pull her from the stage, daring, or should I say, hoping, they try to do something about it. The moment I put her in my arms, everything changed. The attachments I have avoided my whole life become unavoidable. Will this damaged slave be able to replace the shadows in my life? One thing for sure is that I will destroy the entire universe to keep her safe. No one touches what's MINE!

XuL

Brittany

All my dreams and wants were stolen from me in the blink of an eye. Awakening, in the middle of a nightmare, I realize I'm being sold like an animal to be studied and dissected in the name of science. Then tragedy strikes, leaving me abandoned and sick. I am only moments from taking my last breath when strong arms pull me from the darkness. I thought it was a blessing that he had found me, the green man who had haunted my dreams. I let myself believe, for just one moment, I might find a small piece of happiness in this unknown world. But what is the old saying? *'Don't count your chickens until they hatch!'*

A blood sucking parasite is eating me alive, literally, and no matter what, I'm not going to survive this horror story. My body is failing me. I beg him to let me go; I just want the pain to stop, but he won't listen. He holds me down and I struggle weakly against his immense strength, choking as blood fills my lungs. When I can't fight any more, Death opens its arms and invites me in.

XuL

My harsh, brutal features have deterred all females, no matter the species. I long for companionship and love. Then I find her, my Kismet, the only one made just for me. The one precious thing I would worship above all others. But the fates are cruel, especially to a male like me.

I am being forced to destroy the fragile bond that has formed between us, as I have to make the hardest decision of my life. One that will make me lose her either way. I hold her small, struggling body against me. Tears flow down my face as she begs me to stop. My heart is crushed as I watch the light leave her beautiful eyes. Upon her final breath, I vow not even Death will keep what's mine.

SoL

Alana

The question is, do I allow this dark moment in time to rob me of the life I could possibly have here? I have never known such horror or fear. If I hadn't experienced it myself, I would have never believed any other living thing could possibly do this to another. The scars may be gone on the outside now, but they will remain forever in my soul. They tell me I can never go back, all that I have ever known is gone. Where does this leave me in the world of monsters? He beckons me, promising me…the fairytale… the impossible dream. Everything I have ever wanted to hear! But I don't know if I'm strong enough to go forward as long as the shadows of our past pull me backwards.

SoL

I knew she was withholding the truth from me. I had no

idea who I held in my arms until it was almost too late. The moment her true essence was revealed to me, my body reacted, reaching out for the one thing I had been searching for my whole life... my Inamorata. The very mistress of my heart and now that I have finally found her. I will follow her through the sands of time... no matter how long it takes. I will find my way back to her... because she is MINE!

RaZ

Katherine

How do you go on when all of your wants and dreams have been destroyed? My loved ones were snatched right out of my hands, leaving me alone in a world of unknowns and terror. I'm lost in the in-between with no familiar paths to follow until the sound of a heartbeat and a whisper draws me back to the land of the living.

RaZ

The moment I laid eyes upon her face, I knew there would be no distance I wouldn't travel to make her my own. Unknown forces try to steal her from my very arms and even if I have to fight the very essence of her world, the universe, or the very Gods we pray to. Nothing will stop me from making her MINE!

Forsaken

Lucas and Emma
Katherine's parents

The one question she often asks herself is *why*. Why has she never been enough? Why doesn't anyone truly want her? She was reminded daily that she was nothing but a worthless girl and only another mouth to feed. The last time she saw her family was the night they dumped her in a ditch on the side of the road and left her to die.

A kind woman took her out of that ditch and gave her a home. Her new family was every girl's dream until a single poisoned scratch took it all away. Emma was tossed away again, becoming a prisoner and a slave to her circumstances. The one person the Cook enjoyed beating regularly. The day Cook sold her body, all of her hopes and dreams were destroyed. But one fateful night, after fighting for her life, she escapes this, Hell.

He finds her on the brink of death, naked, beaten, and barely alive. She thinks he is the Angel of Death, someone who will save her, but he is a real monster. Did she just trade one Hell for another? Will the memories he steals from her dreams soften his heart enough to make him care for something more than himself? Or will he turn her away, just to *Forsake* her, like all the rest?

Betrayed

Tavish and Eve

It seems the ones we love the most are the first to Betray us! One such Betrayal cost me everything: my home, my dreams, and almost my life. The second I started running, I knew I would never be who I was or may have wanted to be. All of my choices were taken away with two last breaths, hers and then my own.

The dreams of my youth were destroyed because of the selfishness of others. I fear my life will become nothing but a cold existence of shadows and detachment.

The poison consuming my very soul is nothing but an excuse for me to lash out at the unfairness of it all. It's exactly the justification I need to deliver the pain others have inflicted on me my entire life. Will the emotions of my untried youth destroy my future as I'm forced into a world I truly don't understand?

My own mind has become my worst enemy, and my fragile heart can't withstand another break. I know he's a deceiver, a devil in disguise, sent to collect my grieving soul. He is the real monster my mother warned me about under the bed. If I let him, he will destroy me in the end with his mischievous smile and lying angel eyes.

To be loved is the only dream I have left, but we all know Betrayal is the one thing you can always count on to crush you.

Forgotten

Tyberius and Victoria

(DaR's father)

I have known this evil was coming for me my whole life, but that doesn't mean I have looked forward to it! I have run from every sign of the darkness, even to the point of being invisible to the ones around me. I've spent my whole life lurking in the shadows of my family. Keeping myself separate from the ones I love, living my dreams, and wants through their eyes.

I had become so wrapped up in their worlds trying to ensure their happiness that the day he appeared in front of me. I never once questioned what I was supposed to do. The one thing my family could always count on is that I'm loyal to fault. Even though I made sure never to get too attached because I was terrified the darkness would take them also, it will do anything it can to defeat me. My goal is to survive and to finally see the light.

I have prayed to every God, for this to pass me by, only to know they can't answer. This is my destiny. I will suffer agony unlike anything my mind can imagine, but to be worthy of the light. I need to find a way to face this darkness.

I will never show him an ounce of weakness, but I scream silently for help. I refuse to let him win because he wants me here for eternity. A soul withered in ice, and loneliness, Forgotten in this room of horrors.

All the stars line up for us one time or another. I just have to wait my turn.

Tordan

Luna

They stole my dreams, my hopes, my very identity, and I had no idea. Years went by and I did everything I was told, I was always the perfect specimen, and the perfect lab rat. I was dissected, even maimed all in the name of science. Then one day a strange smoky voice entered my head, and I knew things were not as they seemed. He promises me that he will never leave me, but my new memories tell me differently.

Tordan

What is it about that one person that attracts you like no other? My mind can't figure out that riddle, but the moment I laid eyes upon her I knew my life would never be the same. When I finally held her in my arms, I swore I would never be without her again. If they think they will get me to comply by using her to control me, they're right. What they don't know is…I will tear this compound, and all that's in it apart, to protect what's MINE.

Hugo

Miya

I awaken to the touch of cold metal hands and talking holograms. Paralyzed and dependent on the Others. They tell me a story… at first; I refuse to believe. A story of no return and extreme loss, but one of the voices is different. He projects anger and distrust…but his hands… even though cold and hard, are always gentle. I have come to crave the sound of his growls because I know within moments he will hold me in his arms. When my sight returns. I was not prepared to see what he really was, but when he collapsed in front of me, his body failing. Why do I suddenly feel like this is my biggest loss yet?

Hugo

I have done everything in my power to prepare a safe

world for her once I'm gone. I fought my attraction, knowing I was unworthy of her trust, but I crave her like no other. Unfortunately, my mind is no longer my own, and the only way to destroy the monster who has invaded my head is death. All that matters in my end… is that she survives… because I would rather die than share what I know is MINE.

The Playboy and the Waitress

Jenna

I was always told never to forget that I was worth something, too! We all know that every little girl dreams of her knight in shining armor. A man who will ride up and save her from the evil things trying to destroy her. Then, of course, we all know they live happily ever after. My knight was untouchable… A Playboy, a man who stole my heart right out of my chest and with very little effort on his part. Unfortunately, he was also a man whose world I would never fit in. You can take the girl out of the country. You can dress her in nice clothes, have her smile beautifully as you parade her on your arm, but you never really take the country out of the girl. I reach out for the brightest of stars… only for him to leave my heart in pieces, crumbling at my feet.

Dage

I watched her for weeks. Every smile she bestowed on me captured me in a way no others had. Circumstances throw us together over and over and no matter how many times I hold her in my arms, it's never enough. I didn't know what I was missing until she walked away. I know, I can't have them and her… so who will lose?

AvX

Ivy

Why are the last words ever spoken to our loved ones is in anger? I knew the moment I left it was a mistake, but my stubborn pride urged me forward. I've awakened to unimaginable horrors, pain unlike anything the human mind could conceive, until him. Now, I'm too scared to trust my own feelings, as they have only led me astray. I push his kindness away, striking out in a rage of harsh words and unwarranted anger. As this new future is revealed to me, I crumble away inside,… slowly and insidiously. How much more do I have to lose before I realize my sole chance of happiness is standing in front of me?

AvX

She is like a wild animal, cornered and frightened,

unwilling to accept any sort of kindness. A fiery soul trapped inside a mind littered with insecurities and heartache. I ache for a kind word or a gentle touch as my body reacts to her slightest touches. How do I convince her to put aside the pain she has endured and take a chance on the unknown,… on me? The fates put her in my path for a reason, and I will find a way to tame the fire that consumes her.

Sage

SAGE

I was forced to make a decision,...her life for mine. It really was a simple question to answer because at the end of the day, I'm nothing more than a wanna be girl, with the dream of being more.

SCOUT:

She doesn't see her own worth, but I will streak through the cosmos to protect her.

ViN

Ember

I was separated from my parents and a world where the most important thing I had to worry about was my next outfit. Everything I have ever been or will be… torn away abruptly as I'm thrown into what feels like never-ending chaos and confusion. Thrust upon an Alien male who I can't understand and dangers I don't comprehend. How do I cope with the reality of being alone on an alien planet where I'm not wanted?

ViN

I live for the next mission, with absolutely no need for a female of any kind. Until a whiny, ungrateful, high-maintenance one falls literally into my arms. Why does the feel of her small body and the urge to make her smile again confuse me? Fighting the attraction and refusing to be like the others. I walk away from the temptation, so why do her tears haunt me so?

Scout

SAGE

The ultimate betrayal on his face when he sees that plug in my hand shatters my cybernetic heart. Helpless, my world turns to chaos, and I spiral downward, crushed by my very own actions.

SCOUT

Trying to be the hero, I lost it all without even knowing it. The world went on without me. However, our love proved to be stronger, and apparently the gods were not done with me yet. With me gone, an unlikely partnership forms risking it all to bring me back, but will it be me, or something else that emerges.